PRACTICAL
PROJECTS
for the YARD
and GARDEN

PRACTICAL PROJECTS *for the* YARD *and* GARDEN

ATTRACTIVE 2x4 WOODWORKING

PROJECTS <u>ANYONE</u> CAN BUILD

TEXT, DRAWINGS, & PHOTOS BY John Kelsey

PROJECT DESIGN BY Ian J. Kirby

CAMBIUM PRESS

Bethel

PRACTICAL PROJECTS FOR THE YARD AND GARDEN

ISBN 1-892836-19-X
First printing: May 2005
Printed in Canada

Published by
     Cambium Press
     PO Box 909
     Bethel, CT 06801
          tel 203-778-2782 www.CAMBIUMPRESS.biz

Library of Congress Cataloging-in-Publication Data

Kelsey, John, 1946-
 Practical projects for the yard and garden : attractive 2x4 woodworking projects anyone can build / text, drawings, and photos by John Kelsey ; project design and construction by Ian J. Kirby.--1st ed.
     p. cm.
ISBN 1-892836-19-X
1. Outdoor furniture--Design and construction. 2. Garden ornaments and furniture--Design and construction. 3. Woodwork. I. Kirby, Ian J., 1932- II. Title.

TT197.5.O9K48 2005
684.1'8--dc22

                            2005010938

CONTENTS

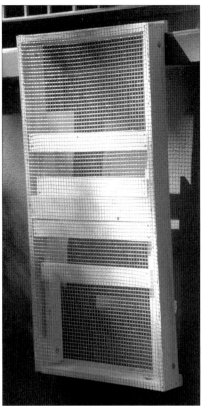

VEGETABLE DRYING TABLE

This handy device folds up and stows away for the off-season

At harvest time, the gardener needs a worktable to wash and dry the vegetables, like this wire-mesh table. Root vegetables need to dry off before they can be taken in for storage.

You'll find the mesh table handy when you're cutting flowers, and also for potting. You can use it for washing down as well as for air-drying. The rest of the year, however, the table probably would only be in the way, if it didn't fold flat for storage. But since it does fold flat,

it's easy to hang it on the wall or tuck it away, and bring it out again at the start of the next gardening season.

BUILDING THE TABLE

1 Cut all the wood. The length of the end rails depends on the width of your wire mesh. If the mesh measures 24 inches, make the end rails $22\frac{3}{4}$ inches long. The length of the cross rails depends on the wood thick-

ness. Trim them to an exact fit in Step 5 below.

2 Make the top frame. Screw the side rails and end rails together to make the rectangular frame. Start at one corner, by clamping one of the end rails up on edge on the worktable. Bring a side rail up to the end rail and clamp it in position, as shown in the photo at far right. Drill clearance holes and make the joint by driving three of the 2-inch screws. Make the other

VEGETABLE DRYING TABLE

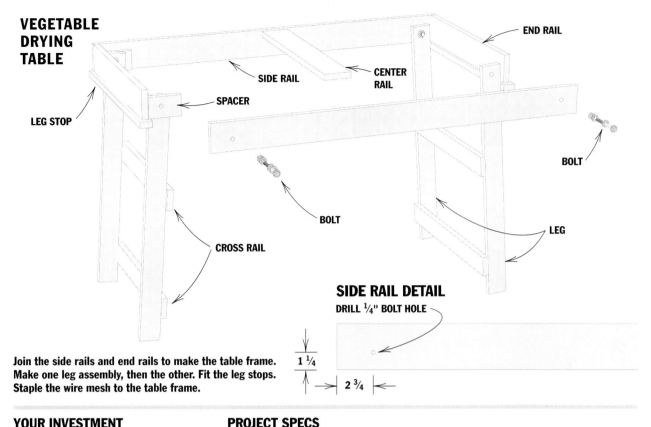

END RAIL

SIDE RAIL

CENTER RAIL

SPACER

LEG STOP

BOLT

BOLT

LEG

CROSS RAIL

SIDE RAIL DETAIL

DRILL ¼" BOLT HOLE

1 ¼

2 ¾

Join the side rails and end rails to make the table frame. Make one leg assembly, then the other. Fit the leg stops. Staple the wire mesh to the table frame.

YOUR INVESTMENT

Time: One evening
Money: $20

SHOPPING LIST

8 feet 1 × 2
24 feet 1 × 3
16 feet 1 × 4
#6 × 2-inch galvanized screws
½-inch hardware cloth, 24 × 48
Two ¼ × 3-inch hex-head bolt
Two ¼ × 2-inch hex-head bolt
¾-inch wire staples

PROJECT SPECS

The vegetable drying table is 48 inches long, 24 inches wide, and 30 inches high.

CUTTING LIST

PART	QTY.	DIMENSIONS	NOTES
Side rail	2	¾ × 3½ × 48	1 × 4
End rail	2	¾ × 3½ × 22 ¾	1 × 4
Leg	4	¾ × 2½ × 30	1 × 3
Cross rail	4	¾ × 2½ × 24	1 × 3; cut to fit
Spacer	2	¾ × 2½ × 4	1 × 3
Leg stop	2	¾ × 1½ × 24 ¼	1 × 2
Center rail	1	¾ × 3½ × 22 ¾	1 × 4

three corners of the frame in the same way. At each corner, screw through the side rail into the end grain of the end rail.

3 Lay out the holes for the leg bolts. A single ¼-inch bolt joins each leg to the table frame. The ¼-inch bolt hole must be correctly positioned, or else the leg won't be able to fold up. As shown in the drawing above, the correct position is 1¼ inches up from the bottom of the rail, and 2¾ inches in from the end of the

Make the top frame. Clamp the side rail and end rail to the worktable. Drill clearance holes, and screw the side rails to the end rails.

Fit one pair of legs. Clamp the first pair of legs in position, inside the table frame. Leave ¹⁄₂-inch pivoting clearance at the end of the leg (above). Drill the bolt hole through the side rail and leg (below). Bolt the leg to the side rail, with a clearance washer between the two parts (right).

Connect the legs with the bottom cross rail. Cut the bottom cross rail to length and screw it to the legs. The rail fits 3 inches up from the end of the leg.

rail. Locate and mark this point on the outside of the side rails.

4 Fit one pair of legs. The folding leg assembly at each end of the table consists of two legs and two cross rails. Spacer blocks at one end of the table allow that leg assembly to fold inside the other one. You'll avoid alignment problems if you complete the first leg assembly, without spacer blocks, before going on to the second. Clamp the legs in folded position inside the side rails, leaving ¹⁄₂-inch pivoting clearance between the end of each leg and the end rail, as shown in the photo at top left. Drill the ¹⁄₄-inch bolt hole through the rail and leg. Bolt each leg to a side rail with the 2-inch bolts. Put a washer under each bolt head and under the nut, and put one extra washer, for clearance, between each leg and side rail.

5 Connect the legs with the bottom cross rail. Measure the outside distance between the legs at the bolt, and subtract ¹⁄₈ inch. Cut the two cross rails to this length. The bottom cross rail fits 3 inches up from the end of the legs. Center the rail across the legs, with ¹⁄₁₆ inch of clearance at either end. Glue and screw the cross rail in position, using two 2-inch screws at either end. Leave the second cross rail aside for now.

6 Fit the second leg assembly. The second leg assembly folds inside the first pair of legs. The spacer blocks create the necessary clearance. Glue the blocks inside the corner of the table frame, as shown in the photo at

right. Then drill and assemble the legs and cross rail as in the previous two steps. The only difference is, put two clearance washers between each leg and spacer block.

7 Fit the upper cross rails. The upper cross rails fit 16 inches up from the bottom of each leg assembly. Glue and screw the upper cross rails to the legs, as in the previous steps. Center each cross rail from side to side so there is $\frac{1}{16}$ inch of clearance to the outside of each leg.

8 Make the leg stops. The leg stops are horizontal pieces of 1×2 fastened underneath the end rails. They limit the splay of the legs when the table is unfolded. The amount of splay is up to you, but one method of making it uniform is shown in the photo below. When you get the leg assemblies in the position you want, butt the leg stops tight against them, then glue and screw the stops to the end rail. Use the 2-inch screws.

9 Fit the center rail. Screw the center rail between the side rails. It goes face-up, so it won't interfere with the folding legs.

10 Make the mesh top. Unroll the $\frac{1}{2}$-inch galvanized wire mesh. It's easy to cut with tin snips or side-cutting pliers, but wear gloves because there are sharp ends. Staple the mesh onto the table frame, as shown in the photo at far right. File off any sharp ends, and you're ready to harvest vegetables. The table doesn't need any finish.

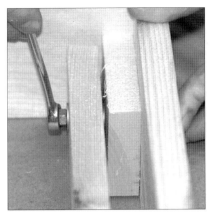

Fit the second leg assembly. Glue the spacer inside the corner of the table frame, then clamp the leg in place, leaving the $\frac{1}{2}$-inch pivot clearance. Drill the bolt hole and bolt the leg in place, with two clearance washers between the leg and spacer (left).

Fit the upper cross rails. Trim the upper cross rails to length and screw them to the leg assemblies.

Make the leg stops. To set the splay of the legs, establish a vertical line with a square and a piece of scrap. Then pull the leg assembly 4 inches off vertical, and butt the leg stop against it (left). Screw the leg stop to the end rail.

Make the mesh top. Staple the $\frac{1}{2}$-inch wire mesh to the table frame. Trim the sharp ends off the mesh, and file off any burrs.

POTTING BENCH

Transplanting is a treat with this sturdy companion

Nothing enhances gardening like a sturdy potting bench with a lot of built-in storage. This bench is a real winner. It can go outdoors or in the garden shed, on the deck, or in the greenhouse. Wherever it's located, you'll have a comfortable place to work, with ample room for tools, pots, bags of peat moss and vermiculite, and anything else you might need for working with your potted plants.

The bench in the photographs was built out of 4/4 rough-sawn pine lumber, which you can find for a reasonable price at a rural sawmill. It's generally a full inch thick, often a bit more. None of the dimensions is critical, so it's easy to transpose the design into 5/4 pine from the home center, which usually comes out around 1⅛ inches thick. If you're building the bench for a sunspace, you might use regular 1× pine, which is ¾ inch thick and results in an elegant lightness. The bench shown is unfinished so it will weather. Rough pine can be stained, and regular 1× pine can be varnished or painted.

Of course, you can make the bench any size you like. The height shown here, 36 inches, is about right for gardeners of average height. If you are tall, make the legs longer, and if you are short, make them shorter. If you aren't sure, check the height of your kitchen counters. If the kitchen counter is comfortable for you, that's the height to use. If it isn't, adjust an inch or two up or down. A small adjustment makes a big difference.

The composite legs are three-layer wood sandwiches. The center layer is assembled from three small pieces of wood, which creates support surfaces for the cross rails and aprons.

POTTING BENCH

Assemble the front legs, apron, and cross rails. Then build the back legs and apron onto the cross rails. Nail the worktop and shelves to this structure.

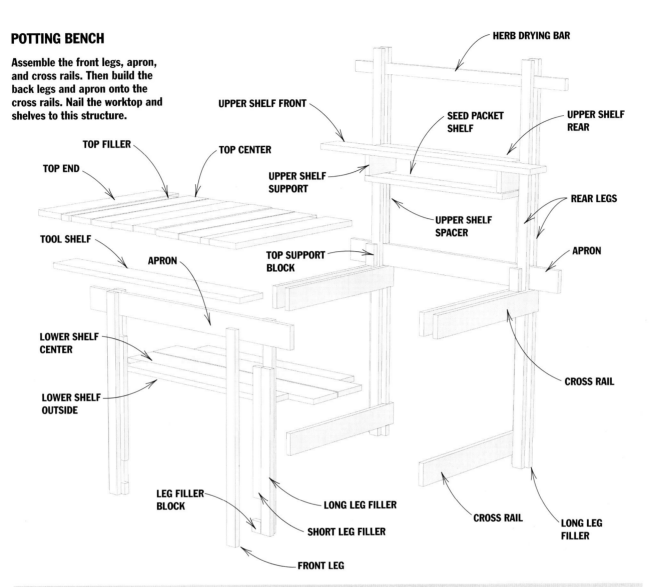

YOUR INVESTMENT

<u>Time:</u> One weekend
<u>Money:</u> $95

SHOPPING LIST

96 feet 1×6 rough-sawn pine
#6 × 2-inch galvanized screws
#8 × 3-inch galvanized screws
2½-inch galvanized finishing nails

PROJECT SPECS

The potting bench is 72 inches high, 48 inches wide, and 28 inches deep. The worktop is 36 inches off the floor.

CUTTING LIST

PART	QTY.	DIMENSIONS	NOTES
Front leg	4	1 × 2 × 35	
Rear leg	4	1 × 2 × 72	
Long leg filler	4	1 × 2 × 29	
Short leg filler	8	1 × 2 × 23	Cut to fit
Leg filler block	4	1 × 2 × 2	Cut to fit
Cross rail	6	1 × 4 × 28	
Apron	2	1 × 4 × 48	
Lower shelf outside	2	1 × 4 × 38	
Lower shelf center	2	1 × 6¾ × 48	
Tool shelf	1	1 × 6 × 48	
Top end	2	1 × 6 × 28	Rip width to fit
Top filler	2	1 × 2 × 24¾	
Top center	6	1 × 5¼ × 28	Rip width to fit
Top support block	2	1 × 2 × 6	
Upper shelf spacer	2	1 × 2 × 14	
Upper shelf support	2	1 × 4 × 8	
Upper shelf front	1	1 × 5 × 48	
Upper shelf rear	1	1 × 4 × 31¾	
Seed packet shelf	1	1 × 5 × 31¾	
Herb drying bar	1	1 × 2 x 48	

Join the front legs and apron. Place the two front legs on the bench top and lay the apron flush with the top of the legs. Set the combination square to 6 inches and draw lines to locate the legs on the apron (left). Drill four pilot holes through the apron, inside the layout lines (right). Angle the holes toward the center of the wood.

This useful strategy allows you to construct serviceable wood joints without having to cut intricately shaped parts.

The slats that make the top of the bench run from front to back instead of from end to end. This allows you to saw useful pieces out of cheap material, which is liable to be too twisted and knotty to yield long boards. You'll find the front-to-back slats easy to sweep clean, too.

Other important details include the setback of the lowest shelf, the top overhang, and the upward extension of the back legs to form shelf supports. The low shelf has enough ceiling room for bags of potting soil, while the setback creates shin room. The top overhangs the long rails by a full 2 inches, so you can get a cleanup bucket right in where you need it. The upward leg extension makes the high shelves a stable part of the bench structure, so clay pots won't teeter off.

BUILDING THE POTTING BENCH

1 Join the front legs and apron. Once you've cut all the wood, begin by assembling two front legs to one apron piece, to make a U-shaped assembly. The trick is keeping the legs square to the apron. The front legs are set in 6 inches from the ends of the apron. The photo sequence across these two pages shows the steps of laying out the intersection, drilling pilot holes for screws, spreading glue, and driving the screws home. Use the longest screws that will fit without poking through the other side.

2 Square up the assembly. Drive one screw through the apron into each leg, then measure the width of the top and bottom and both diagonals. If the widths are equal, and the two diagonals are equal, the assembly is square. If it's not square, pull the pieces into position before the glue sets, then drive the remaining screws.

3 Join the front legs and top cross rails. Drill three pilot holes through both ends of four cross rails. Smear a bead of glue on the wood, then clamp the rails to the front legs and apron. Pull the rails up tight to the bottom surface of the apron as shown in the bottom photo on page 13. Drive three of the 3-inch screws through each joint.

4 Join the bottom cross rails. The top of the lower rails is 6 inches off the floor. Measure 6 inches up the inside face of both legs, then glue and screw the cross rails in position.

5 Assemble the legs. The long leg filler piece fits tight against the top cross rail and extends to the floor. The short leg filler fits tight between the top and bottom cross rails. Hold these pieces in position to mark their length, then saw them so they fit snugly between the rails. Attach each filler to the front legs with glue and four of the 2-inch screws. Finally, saw the leg filler

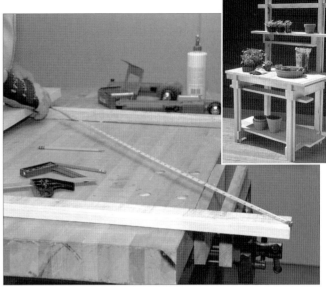

Square up the assembly. Drive a single screw into each of the two joints. Bury the heads in the wood (left). Measure the width top and bottom, then measure the two diagonals from the outside bottom corner of the leg to the inside corner of the apron (right). Adjust the assembly until the diagonals are equal, then drive the remaining screws.

BELT AND SUSPENDERS

The drawing on page 11 shows neither the many galvanized construction screws that hold the potting bench together, nor the glue.

In general there are at least two, but no more than four, screws through every wood-to-wood intersection. And there's also a fat bead of yellow glue everywhere that two parts lie across one another.

Whether there is room for two screws or three or four screws, always space them as widely apart as possible, and angle them so they're better able to resist stress.

Clamp the mating parts tightly together before driving the construction screws. Four 12-inch clamps, like the ones shown in the photographs at right, are all you need for a construction like this: glue, clamp, and screw each joint before moving on.

Use the longest screws the thickness of the wood will accept, short of the screw point emerging on the other side.

Spread yellow glue where the parts fit together. Spread it on all the mating surfaces. Pine is so soft that you don't need to drill pilot holes, except when you're within a couple of inches of the end of the wood. Clamp up first, then drill just through the top piece, using a regular twist bit that's smaller than the screw's thread diameter.

Surely two or three galvanized construction screws at every intersection would be strong enough to hold a bench together? Well, probably. But, like the gentleman who wears both belt and suspenders, the glue is insurance. It would keep the parts together even if the screws were to work loose.

Spread yellow glue where the parts will fit together.

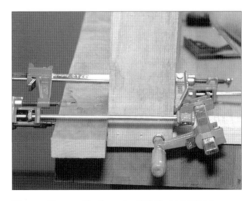

Clamp the mating parts tightly together so they don't shift while you drive the screws.

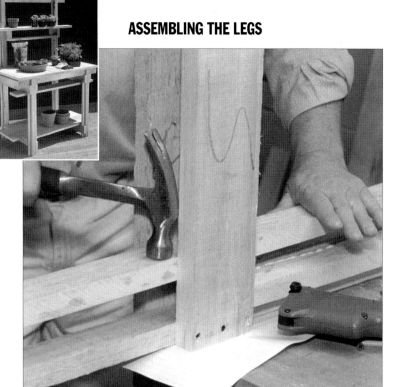

ASSEMBLING THE LEGS

Run a bead of glue along both filler pieces, then press the leg into place. The leg fits tightly between the two cross rails.

COMPOSITE LEG

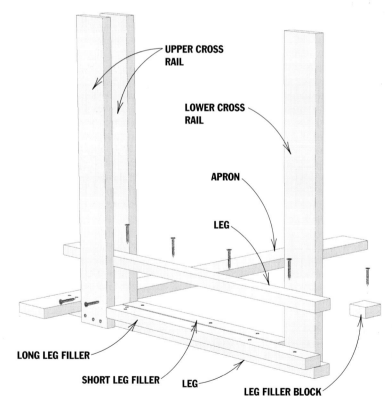

- UPPER CROSS RAIL
- LOWER CROSS RAIL
- APRON
- LEG
- LONG LEG FILLER
- SHORT LEG FILLER
- LEG
- LEG FILLER BLOCK

Clamps hold the leg while you drive pairs of screws into the filler pieces.

Complete the front legs. Driving two more screws through the cross rail and into the leg makes the construction incredibly strong.

The composite leg is a four-piece wood sandwich assembled around the apron and cross rails. The leg filler pieces support the two top cross rails. Trim the short leg filler to a tight fit between the top and bottom cross rails. Glue and screw all the parts as you assemble the leg.

blocks to just fill the space below the bottom cross rails. A little glue and a single screw is enough to hold each filler block in place.

6 Complete the front legs. Fit the remaining leg piece between the cross rails and clamp it in place. Screw through it into the apron and leg fillers. Finally, drive a couple of 3-inch screws through the outside face of each cross rail into the side of the leg piece, as shown at bottom left. These screws make the construction very strong.

7 Construct the rear legs. Despite their extra length, the rear legs are also composites that go together in exactly the same way as the front legs, as shown at above right. Glue and screw the rear leg parts to the cross rails as you go along. The rear apron slides in last. This completes the structure of the potting bench.

8 Fit the lower shelves. Crosscut the four boards for the lower shelf and nail them in place, as shown at right. Don't make the fit too tight. It's better to leave a little space between the boards, so the wood can swell if it gets wet. Screw the narrow tool shelf to the underside of the cross rails. You'll be surprised by how handy this shelf is when you're working.

9 Make the tabletop. Screw the two small support blocks to the rear legs, then fit and nail the two top fillers in place. Add the two top end boards, which should fit flush with the ends of the aprons. Fill in the center

Construct the rear legs. Make sure the short leg fillers fit tightly between the top and bottom cross rails. Glue and screw the composite legs together.

Fit the lower shelves. You can get at the tool shelf and at least one of the boards for the lower shelf while the potting table is still on its back on the worktable. Stand it upright to complete nailing the shelf parts in place.

space. If all the boards are not the same width, arrange them in a pattern. Drive galvanized finishing nails through the top boards into the aprons.

10 Fit the upper shelves. Fit the upper shelf spacers into the slot between the rear legs. Screw the upper shelf supports to the rear legs. Cut the upper shelf rear to fit between the rear legs and nail it in place. Nail the upper shelf front onto the supports. Nail the seed packet shelf onto the bottom of the shelf supports. Finally, nail the herb drying bar between the rear legs.

TRUG

Traditional wooden basket helps harvest your tomatoes

Oh, it's so romantic to traipse through the garden with your trug slung over your arm, gathering a bountiful harvest of beans, rhubarb or daisies. The bees buzz and the dewdrops glisten in the morning sunshine. The rustic trug allows you to imagine, just for a moment, that you've been transported to a simpler time with nothing more important to do than harvest your tomatoes.

As a gardening tool, the trug, or wooden basket, has a couple of singular virtues. The base is broad, so it's almost impossible to upset. The loose weave is washable under the garden hose. The high handle is easy to pick up. And the trug is simple to make, despite the apparent complexity of its woven basket.

Trugs are traditional British woodcraft, though the one shown here is not an authentic copy of something traditional, but a contemporary rendition.

The basket is woven from slats sawn lengthwise off the edge of a 2×4, a maneuver that requires a table saw or a band saw. The curve is jigsawn or bandsawn into the edges of regular 1×4 pine boards. Nails and screws hold the trug together.

Weave the basket. Lay the center weft across four long warps (left). Drop the remaining three warps on top, then weave in the second and third wefts, over and under (center). Add the fourth and fifth wefts at either end of the panel (right).

BUILDING THE TRUG

1 Cut the wood. To make the slats, begin with a 24-inch knot-free length of 2×4. Set up the table saw rip fence for a thin cut, $\frac{1}{8}$ inch or a little less. Reduce the entire 2×4 to thin slats—you need 11 total.

2 Weave the basket. The basket of the trug is a wooden weaving that consists of seven long slats, or warps, crossed by five short slats, or wefts. Lay the seven warps flat on the worktable, then remove three of them, as shown in the photo at top left. Center a weft across the four warps, then replace the three warps you just removed. Now weave a pair of wefts over and under on either side of the center warp. This will stabilize the "fabric." Then add another

TRUG

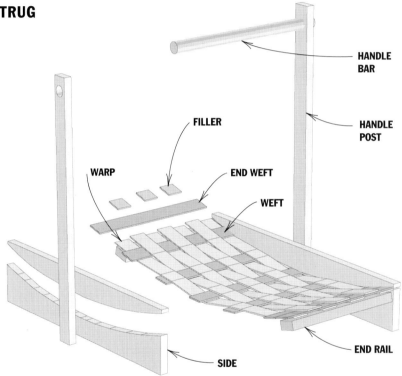

Weave the basket of the trug. Jigsaw the sides, connect them with the end rails, then nail the woven basket to them. Drill the handle posts and screw them to the trug sides. Nail the handle bar to the handle posts.

YOUR INVESTMENT

<u>Time:</u> One evening
<u>Money:</u> $5

SHOPPING LIST

4 feet 1×4 pine
2 feet 2×4 pine or fir
6 feet 1×2 pine
1-inch nails
1-inch brass linoleum nails
2-inch galvanized siding nails
1¼-inch galvanized screws

PROJECT SPECS

The trug is 24 inches long, 12 inches wide, and 24 inches high.

CUTTING LIST

PART	QTY.	DIMENSIONS	NOTES
Warp	7	$\frac{1}{8} \times 1\frac{1}{2} \times 24$	Rip from 2×4
Weft	7	$\frac{1}{8} \times 1\frac{1}{2} \times 12$	Rip from 2×4
Filler	6	$\frac{1}{8} \times 1\frac{1}{2} \times 1\frac{1}{2}$	Rip from 2×4
Side	2	$\frac{3}{4} \times 3\frac{1}{2} \times 24$	1×4
End	2	$\frac{3}{4} \times 1\frac{1}{2} \times 10\frac{5}{8}$	1×2
Handle post	2	$\frac{3}{4} \times 1\frac{1}{2} \times 24$	1×2
Handle bar	1	1 dia. × 18	dowel

pair of wefts, one at either end of the panel. Once all five wefts are interwoven with the seven warps, you can space them any way you like.

3 Make the curved sides. Bend one of the long warp slats to lay out the curve in the sides, as shown below. At the center, the curve is 1¾ inches deep. Jigsaw the first side, then trace its shape onto the second one and jigsaw it too. Make these saw-cuts as single sweeps without any back-tracking, and keep the curved scraps, because you'll nail them onto the trug in Step 7 below. Ending up with a one-piece scrap is more important than precision.

4 Make the ends. The ends are short pieces of 1×2 nailed between the sides. The top face of the ends comes flush with the jigsawn curve. Hold the ends in place and once you see how they go, nail them to the sides with two of the 2-inch siding nails at each joint, as shown in the photo at bottom left.

5 Nail the wefts to the sides. Press the woven wood onto the curved sides. It should fit nicely between them, with the ends of the wefts on the sawn curves, as shown at bottom right. Starting at the center, tack the wefts onto the sides. Drive two 1-inch nails into each weft.

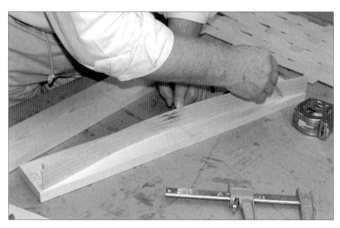

Make the sides. Tap a nail near each end of the side, and bend a long warp slat against the nails. Trace this curve onto the wood (left). Then jigsaw the curve (right).

Make the ends. Nail the ends between the curved sides. The face of the end piece follows the jigsawn curve.

Nail the wefts to the sides. Fit the woven wood into the trug and nail the ends of the wefts to the sides.

Fill in the ends of the warps. Slip the end weft into the basket, and fill the gaps with the filler pieces (above). Nail the warps to the ends (right).

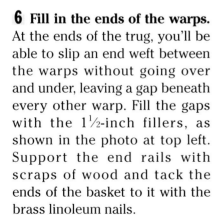

Replace the curved scrap. Fit the curved scrap from whence it came and nail it to the sides, trapping the woven basket.

Make the handle. Center and square the handle posts on the sides of the trug (top). Screw the posts to the sides from underneath (above). Insert the dowel handle and tack it in place (below). Trim the handle ends with a handsaw.

6 Fill in the ends of the warps. At the ends of the trug, you'll be able to slip an end weft between the warps without going over and under, leaving a gap beneath every other warp. Fill the gaps with the 1½-inch fillers, as shown in the photo at top left. Support the end rails with scraps of wood and tack the ends of the basket to it with the brass linoleum nails.

7 Replace the curved scrap. Fit the curved scraps from the jig-sawing operation in Step 3 back onto the sides, covering the ends of the wefts. Nail the curved scrap onto the sides, using the 2-inch siding nails, as shown in the lower left photo.

8 Make the handle. The handle consists of two upright posts spanned by a dowel handle bar. Begin by drilling a 1-inch hole through the two handle posts, 2½ inches from the top of the posts. Next, fasten the handle posts to the sides of the trug with three screws from inside and underneath, plus a fourth screw through the curved scrap. Finally, insert the handle bar and retain it with brass nails, as shown in the photo at right.

TOOL HOUSE

A handy place to store all your shovels,
hoes and rakes

Storage for garden tools is always a problem. The tools you need in the springtime get buried behind the tools you used all winter. With the best of intentions, there's an impenetrable thicket of handles that interferes with doing your chores.

The answer is a special house or cabinet for the garden tools. This tool house is a tall, flat box that stands against the outside wall of your house or garage nearest the garden itself. If you've been thinking that you need a full-scale garden shed,

consider making this simple tool house instead.

The tool house rests on a couple of bricks or blocks on the ground. It's fastened to the building with a couple of nails or screws through the back. The hinged doors open wide so you can easily get at what you need, and they close tight against winter weather. The board-and-rail construction allows you to assemble the back, sides and doors from narrow boards.

The construction of the tool house is straightforward. It's held together with glue and screws. Its sides do have to be sawn at an angle to meet with the pitched roof. The steps below show laying out and cutting the angle with a hand saw, after you assemble the sides. If you've got a power saw, the task is that much easier.

The tool house doors have a Z-shaped rail and brace on the inside. This is a very useful way of making a stiff panel out of narrow boards, one that you can use in other applications.

The inside of this tool house measures 9 inches deep, 34 inches wide, and 6 feet high. Of course the size of the box can be adjusted, though if you make it deeper than about 12 inches or wider than 48 inches, you would need to add rafters to help support the roof. You can make it narrower or shallower without any change in construction, and there is something elegant about keeping cabinets like this down to their minimum useful size. If you like to garden with nothing but your custom-made European hoe, you could make the house exactly big enough to store that one tool.

BUILDING THE TOOL HOUSE

1 Cut the wood. The tool house, as shown, is made of solid wood with a plywood roof. When you buy the 1×6 lumber for the sides, back and doors, choose 6-foot or 12-foot boards, not 8-footers. Begin by sawing all the wood to the sizes given in the cutting list. Since the back is neither structural nor visible, it's a good place to use up knotty and twisted wood. You could substitute a piece of ⅝-inch CDX plywood measuring 33 inches × 70 inches for the six back boards, and T1-11 siding for the plywood roof, but the sides and doors look best as solid wood.

2 Make the first side. Each side of the tool house consists of two 1x6 boards connected by three glued-and-screwed rails. The bottom side rail is 6 inches up from the end of the boards; the middle side rail is 40 inches up, and the top rail, which is discussed in Step 3, establishes

TOOL HOUSE

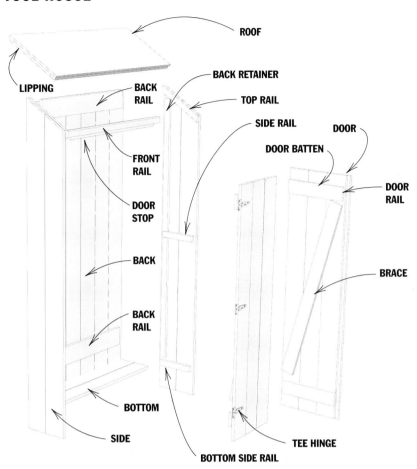

Begin by making the tool house sides and attaching the back retainers. Make the back and screw it to the sides. Add the front rail and the bottom, install the roof, then make the doors. Hang the doors, then install the tool house against your house or garage.

YOUR INVESTMENT

Time: All day
Money: $80

SHOPPING LIST

32 feet 1×2 pine
16 feet 1×4 pine
16 feet 1×5 pine
96 feet 1×6 pine
⅙ sheet ½-inch CDX plywood
#6 × 1 ¼-inch galvanized screws
#6 × 1 ⅝-inch galvanized screws
#6 × 2-inch galvanized screws
Six 4-inch galvanized tee hinges
One 3-inch barrel bolt

PROJECT SPECS

The tool house is 79 inches high, 43 inches wide at the roof, and 15 inches deep at the roof.

CUTTING LIST

PART	QTY.	DIMENSIONS	NOTES
Side	4	$\frac{3}{4} \times 5\frac{1}{2} \times 78$	1×6
Side rail	4	$\frac{3}{4} \times 1\frac{1}{2} \times 9\frac{1}{2}$	1×2
Top rail	2	$\frac{3}{4} \times 1\frac{1}{2} \times 15$	1×2; cut to fit
Back retainer	4	$\frac{3}{4} \times 1\frac{1}{2} \times 36$	1×2; cut to fit
Back	6	$\frac{3}{4} \times 5\frac{1}{2} \times 70$	1×6
Back rail	2	$\frac{3}{4} \times 4\frac{1}{2} \times 30$	1×5
Bottom	2	$\frac{3}{4} \times 4\frac{1}{2} \times 35$	1×5; cut to fit
Front rail	1	$\frac{3}{4} \times 1\frac{1}{2} \times 36$	1×2; cut to fit
Roof	1	$\frac{1}{2} \times 16 \times 43$	CDX plywood
Lipping		$\frac{3}{4} \times 1\frac{1}{2} \times 72$	1×2; cut to fit
Door	6	$\frac{3}{4} \times 5\frac{1}{2} \times 63$	1×6
Door rail	4	$\frac{3}{4} \times 3\frac{1}{2} \times 16$	1×4
Brace	2	$\frac{3}{4} \times 3\frac{1}{2} \times 48$	1×4
Door stop	1	$\frac{3}{4} \times 1\frac{1}{2} \times 32$	1×2; cut to fit
Door batten	1	$\frac{3}{4} \times 1\frac{1}{2} \times 63$	1×2

Make the first side. Center the bottom side rail on the side boards. Use a piece of scrap to gauge the margins for the back and door.

Attach the top rail. The carpenter's protractor establishes the 30-degree angle of the top side rail.

Trim the side and top rail. Saw the side to the angle established by the top side rail (above). Trim the ends of the rail flush with the sides (right).

the pitch of the roof. Start with the bottom side rail. Square a line 6 inches up from the end of the side boards, spread glue on the side rail, and clamp it in place. It should be centered from side to side, leaving margins the thickness of the back boards and door, as shown in the photo at top left. Drive four of the 1¼-inch screws through the side rail into the two side boards. Attach the center side rail to the two side boards in the same way.

3 **Attach the top rail.** The top rail establishes the 30-degree pitch of the tool house roof. Use a speed square or a carpenter's protractor, as shown in the photo at left, to locate the top rail on the side. Spread glue on it, clamp it, and screw it to the two side boards with six of the 1¼-inch screws.

4 **Trim the side and top rail.** The top rail is the template for sawing the side boards to match the pitch of the roof. Saw directly along the edge of the top rail, as shown in the photos at left. Then trim the ends of the top rail to match the sides. If you deviate from the line established by the rail, rasp the excess wood off with a Surform.

5 **Make the second side.** The second side of the tool house is the same as the first side, except of opposite handedness. Attach the bottom and middle side rails. Keep the completed side panel close at hand when you attach the top rail, so you can be sure its pitch is opposite, as shown in the photo at the top of the facing page.

6 Attach the back retainers.
The back retainers provide a means for attaching the back panel to the tool house sides. Cut them to fit from 1×2 wood. The bottom retainer fits between the two side rails, leaving a gap for the tool house bottom, as shown in the center photo at right. The top retainer fits between the middle side rail and the top rail. While you could cut an angle at its top end, it's not necessary to do so. Glue and screw the back retainers to the side boards. Use a piece of scrap wood as a gauge to set the retainers in from the back edge of the side panels. Drive four of the 1¼-inch screws through each retainer.

7 Make the back. The back consists of six boards held together by two back rails. There should be a little space between the back boards, so the wood can move with changes in the weather. The top back rail becomes the nailer for the roof, so it has to overlap the ends of the boards by 1½ inches, as shown in the photo below at right. The bottom back rail has to clear the bottom of the tool house, so locate it about 6 inches up the back. Center each rail from side to side, leaving a margin of an inch at either side. This margin has to be wide enough to clear the back retainers. Screw the two back rails to the six back boards with two or three 1¼-inch screws through each rail into each board.

8 Attach the back to the sides.
Making the initial connection between the back and sides is somewhat awkward, but once

Make the second side. Keep the first side nearby when you make the second side, to be sure one is right-handed and the other left-handed.

Attach the back retainers. Fit the back retainers between the side rails, leaving a gap for the bottom (left). The gauge block, behind thumb, holds the space for the tool house back.

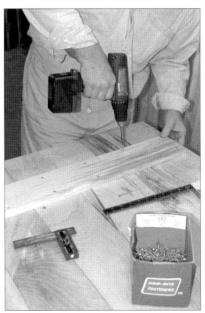

Make the back. The top back rail extends beyond the six back boards by the width of the 1×2 gauge strip (left). Screw the bottom back rail to the back boards (above).

Attach the back to the sides. Stand the first side in position on the back. The top edge of the back rail extends just beyond the top side rail (left). Attach the back with two screws driven from below (center). Turn the assembly over to attach the second side, and drive screws along both edges of the back (below).

Shape the top back rail. Rasp a flat along the edge of the top back rail. The flat makes a nailing surface for the roof.

Make the bottom. Screw the two bottom boards to the bottom side rails.

the first two screws are in, the whole process becomes easy. Stand one side in position on the back, as shown in the photo at top left. The top edge of the top back rail should extend just beyond the top side rails. Draw a layout line on the back, remove the side, and drill two clearance holes through the back where the side will fit, one near the top and the other near the bottom. Then run a bead of glue along the back retainer and

replace the side on the back. Now reach up from below to drive two 2-inch screws through the back and into the back retainer, as shown in the photo at top center. These two screws give the construction enough stability for you to turn it over on the worktable and attach the second side with glue and a couple of screws, as shown in the photo directly above. Then, go all along both edges of the back and screw it to the retainers.

9 Shape the top back rail. The top back rail needs a nailing flat where the roof will fit. In the previous step you let the top back rail extend just beyond the top side rails. Now rasp the corner off the top back rail, to create a flat that is in line with the pitch of the top side rails, as shown in the top right photo.

10 Make the bottom. The bottom of the tool house consists of two 1×5 boards screwed onto

the bottom side rails. Since the precise width of the tool house depends on the width of your 1×6 lumber, the length of the bottom boards has to be cut to fit. After you've screwed the bottom boards to the bottom side rails, also screw through the back into the edge of the bottom.

11 Make the front rail. The front rail ties the top of the tool house together, and also allows the door to clear the front edge of the roof. Hold the top rail in place, its bottom edge flush with the tail of the top side rail. Mark and saw it to length, then glue and screw it to the top of the sides and the ends of the top side rails. Finally, rasp its top edge flush with the pitch of the roof, as shown in the photo at right.

12 Install the roof. The roof is a piece of exterior-grade plywood or T1-11 siding. It's screwed to the pitched sides of the tool house, and to the front and top back rails. Since plywood isn't very flat, glue and screw a 1×2 lipping to the exposed three sides of the roof before you attach it to the tool house, as shown in the photo at bottom right. If you set the lipping back ¼ inch from the edge of the plywood, it not only makes a shadow reveal, it also makes a drip edge that sheds water. Center the roof from side to side and fasten it to the tool house with 1¼-inch screws.

13 Make the first door. The doors are made of the same 1×6 lumber as the back of the tool house. Each door consists of

Make the front rail. Screw the front rail to the top side rail, then rasp its edge into line with the pitch of the roof. Use a stick to gauge your progress.

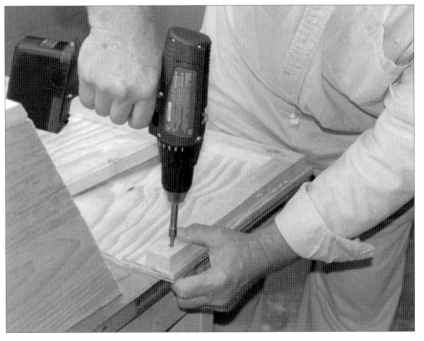

Install the roof. Glue and screw the lipping to the plywood roof, then screw the roof to the tool house.

three boards connected by two rails and a brace. Fit three of the door boards tight together on the worktable. Lay the diagonal brace across the three boards, as shown in the photo at left below. Center the brace from end to end, and bring its corners just inside the edges of the door boards. Attach the brace by driving six of the 1¼-inch screws into each door board. Space the screws as widely apart as possible. Center the two door rails on the door, 3 inches up from either end, and attach them with four screws into each door board, as shown in the photo at bottom left.

14 Make the second door. The doors are strongest when the brace runs down toward the hinge side, as shown in the photo on page 20. This means the two doors should be of opposite handedness. Make the second door with the first door laying on the worktable as reference, so that one brace runs one way and the other runs the other way, as shown in the photo below.

15 Hang the doors. Each door hangs on three tee hinges. Screw the hinges to the doors while they are still on the worktable, then hang the doors on the tool house. Locate the top and bottom hinges so the screws go into the door rails. Screw the narrow leaf of the tee hinges to the edges of the tool house sides, as shown in the top photo on the

Make the first door. Screw the diagonal door brace across the door boards (above). Center the door rails 3 inches in from the ends of the door (below).

Make the second door. The braces on the two doors should run in opposite directions, with the bottom of each brace on the hinge side of its door.

facing page. To create clearance, lay a stick of scrap on the bottom of the tool house, then rest the bottom door rail on it.

16 Make the door stop. The door stop creates a surface for mounting the strike of the barrel bolt, and incidentally fills the gap at the top of the doors. It's screwed to the back of the front rail. Cut the length of the door stop to match the distance between the top side rails. Its width depends on the height of your doors, and on how much gap you have to fill.

17 Make the door batten. The door batten is a vertical strip attached to the outside edge of one door. When this door is bolted shut, the batten catches and holds the other door closed. It also covers any vertical gap between the doors. Screw the batten to the door from the inside.

18 Mount the barrel bolt. The barrel bolt mounts vertically at the top of the battened door. Mount the strike on the door stop, as shown in the photo below at right.

19 Install the tool house. To delay rotting, the sides of the tool house should rest on bricks or concrete blocks. Adjust the blocks until the tool house stands vertically against the wall of the building. Then nail or screw through the back into the wall. If the building has board-and-batten siding, shakes, clapboards or shingles, you can add matching trim to the tool house roof and sides. Paint it or stain it to match the building.

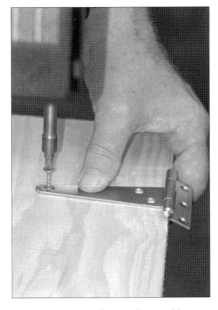

Hang the doors. Screw the tee hinges to the doors (above), then screw them to the tool house sides (right).

Make the door stop. Screw the door stop to the back of the front rail. Make it just wide enough to fill the gap above the doors.

Mount the barrel bolt. Attach the batten to one of the doors, then mount the barrel bolt on the same door. Screw the strike to the door stop above the door.

GARDEN CART

This big and useful box on wheels bounces over any terrain

After 20 years of hard service, the axle supports rusted out and the plywood bottom rotted away, and my old garden cart bit the dust. Time to make a new one.

The old cart came out of a kit of metal hardware and plywood. I wanted the new cart to be all wood, except for the wheels and axles. It had to be larger, and perhaps better overall.

The new cart would have to be sturdy enough for every gar-den chore: moving tools and flats of plants and balled shrubs, loads of earth and compost, bales of hay and peat moss, piles of rocks, firewood, and leaves. It should have soft pneumatic tires, for easy rolling over gravel and uneven ground. The box ends had to be angled, not only for dumping, but also for foot clearance while toiling up a steep grade. Not least, I wanted to use up a leftover sheet of T1-11 siding. T1-11 is tough mat-erial, and it's not bad looking.

If you're like me, you're liable to leave your garden cart out-doors all summer. Even though the T1-11 is made with water-proof glue, the wood will rot if rain water pools on it. There-fore, I cut the cart's bottom panel a little bit short of the ends, for drainage. If you haul a lot of loose sand, you might con-sider this detail a bug instead of a valuable feature.

Be sure to use Titebond type

GARDEN CART

Assemble the box by gluing and screwing panels of T1-11 siding to the frame pieces. Then make the axle assembly, and finally add the top trim, handles, and legs.

AXLE DETAIL

Nuts and washers space the wheel on the threaded-rod axle. Two nuts jammed together hold the wheel on the axle.

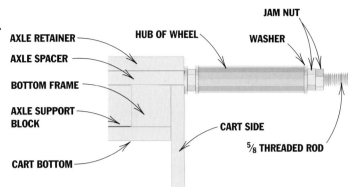

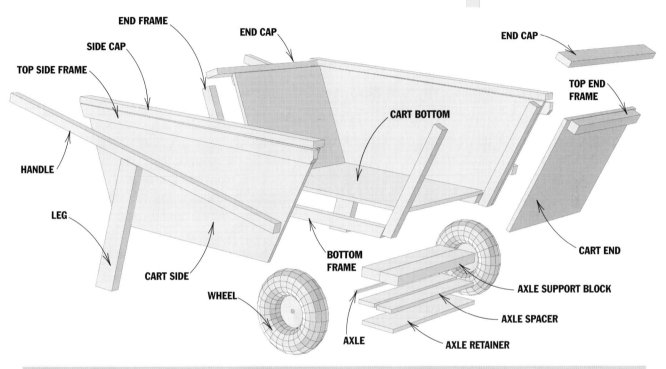

YOUR INVESTMENT

<u>Time:</u> One weekend

<u>Money:</u> $35 for wood; $35 for wheels and hardware

SHOPPING LIST

F32 feet 2×4
One sheet ⅝-inch or ¹⁹/₃₂-inch
  T1-11 siding
16 feet 1×3 pine
3 feet ⅝ × 16 NC threaded rod
Six ⅝-inch washers and nuts
Two 13-inch pneumatic wheels
  with ⅝-inch ball-bearing hub
#6 × 1⅝-inch galvanized screws
#6 × 2-inch galvanized screws
#8 × 2½-inch galvanized screws

PROJECT SPECS

The cart measures 60 inches from handles to far end, 25 inches high, and 36 inches wide at the axle.

CUTTING LIST

PART	QTY.	DIMENSIONS	NOTES
Cart side	2	$^{19}/_{32} \times 18 \times 48$	T1-11 siding
End frame	4	$1\frac{1}{2} \times 1\frac{1}{2} \times 22$	Rip from 2×4
Bottom frame	2	$1\frac{1}{2} \times 1\frac{1}{2} \times 29\frac{1}{2}$	Rip from 2×4
Cart end	2	$^{19}/_{32} \times 19\frac{1}{4} \times 23\frac{1}{2}$	T1-11 siding
Cart bottom	1	$^{19}/_{32} \times 23\frac{1}{2} \times 29\frac{5}{8}$	T1-11 siding
Axle support block	2	$1\frac{1}{2} \times 3\frac{1}{2} \times 20\frac{1}{4}$	2×4
Axle spacer	2	$^{19}/_{32} \times 3 \times 24\frac{3}{4}$	T1-11 siding
Axle retainer	1	$^{19}/_{32} \times 6 \times 24\frac{3}{4}$	T1-11 siding
Handle	2	$1\frac{1}{2} \times 1\frac{1}{2} \times 60$	Rip from 2×4
Leg	2	$1\frac{1}{2} \times 3\frac{1}{2} \times 15$	Bevel one end
Top end frame	2	$1\frac{1}{2} \times 1\frac{1}{2} \times 21$	Trim to fit
Top side frame	2	$1 \times 2 \times 52$	Trim to fit
End cap	2	$1 \times 2\frac{1}{2} \times 46$	Trim to fit
Side cap	2	$1 \times 2\frac{1}{2} \times 32$	Trim to fit

Add the end frames. Glue and clamp the end frames to the cart sides. Align the bottom of the side with the inside corner of the end frame. Drill pilot holes and screw the parts together.

Make the cart sides. Saw the T1-11 diagonally across the first decorative panel on each edge of the sheet. Clamp the siding to the worktable to saw these lines.

Bevel the frame ends. Use a scrap of T1-11 to lay out the slot between end frame and bottom frame. Saw the slot. Also saw the end frame flush with the cart side.

2 glue, or its equivalent, for water resistance. Spread glue everywhere two wood surfaces fit together. The screws are all galvanized, and you must always drill pilot holes.

If you buy 2×2 wood for the frames and handles, you can saw all the rest of the parts, including the T1-11 siding, with a shark-tooth handsaw like the one shown in the top photo. Otherwise, you'll need access to a table saw to cut these parts lengthwise out of 2×4 studs.

BUILDING THE GARDEN CART

1 Make the cart sides. Saw two pieces of T1-11 measuring 18 inches by 48 inches, with the decorative grooves running across the short dimension. Use the grooves, which are 7½ inches apart, to lay out the slope of the cart ends. As shown at top left, draw a diagonal line from groove to groove across the first panel of siding. Clamp the sheet to the worktable so the layout line is just beyond the

table edge. If you have a portable circular saw, you can fire it up to saw this line, or else you can do it with a handsaw, as shown in the photo at left. Saw both ends of the cart side. Lay out the second side by tracing along the first one.

2 Add the end frames. Saw an 8-foot 2×4 in half lengthwise to make 2×2 material for the cart's structural frame. Crosscut one piece into four 22-inch lengths. Glue and clamp them along the angled cut on the plain face of the cart sides, so the inside corner of the wood comes flush with the bottom of the cart side, as shown above. Screw through the T1-11 into the end frames.

3 Make the bottom frames. Use the other half of the 2×4 you just sawed to make the two 29¼-inch bottom frames. The bottom frame pieces should just fit between the end frames, flush with the bottom edge of the T1-11 cart side. Drive eight screws through the T1-11 cart sides into each bottom frame.

Fit the end panels. Fit the end panels into the slots between the frame pieces. Glue and screw both ends to one cart side (above). Glue and clamp the other cart side in place, and screw the assembly together (right).

4 Bevel the frame ends. The ends of the bottom frames need to be beveled parallel to the end frames, leaving a ⅝-inch gap for the T1-11 cart ends. Lay a scrap of T1-11 against the end frames to draw a layout line, as shown at bottom left on the facing page. Cut the bevel with your handsaw as shown at bottom right on the facing page. Similarly, trim the protruding bottom corner off the end frames.

5 Make the cart ends. Two cart ends come out of one 48-inch width of T1-11 that's 19¼ inches long. Saw the siding down the middle of the center groove. Then saw the partial grooves off both edges of each piece, leaving three full panes of siding. Our end panels finished 23½ inches wide.

6 Fit the end panels. The two end panels connect the sides of the cart. Lay one cart side on the worktable and spread glue on the end frames. Fit the first panel into the slot between the end frame and bottom frame. Align the panel with the cart side. Drill pilot holes and screw through the end panel into the end frame. Attach the second end panel to the cart side in the same way. Finally, spread glue on the end frames of the other cart side, plug it into place, and screw the cart body together.

7 Add the cart bottom. The cart bottom is also T1-11 siding, with the smooth back facing up. It's glued and screwed to the bottom frame. The dimensions given in the cutting list fit tightly from side to side, with ¼-inch of clearance in length. This clearance creates narrow slots at either end, which allow water to drain out of the cart. If you don't want your cart to leak, mark and cut the bottom to a tight fit. If you were to bevel the ends of the bottom to match the slope of the cart ends, you could bring the box within caulking distance of watertight.

8 Make the axle support blocks. The wheel axle is a 36-inch length of ⅝-inch threaded rod. It's supported by two lengths of 2×4 glued and

Make the axle support blocks. Glue and screw two lengths of 2×4 to the cart bottom. These blocks should fit tightly between the bottom frames.

screwed to the cart bottom. If you can't find a single 36-inch length of threaded rod, you can use two shorter lengths instead. Either way, the construction is the same. Saw the two axle support blocks and trim the to a tight fit between the bottom frames. The first axle support block fits 6 inches back from the front end of the cart. The second one fits tightly against it. Spread glue on the cart bottom as well as on the support blocks, and also spread glue in between the two blocks. Tap them into place, clamp them together side to

Complete the frame. Glue and screw reinforcing frame pieces around the top edges of the cart body, then saw the protrusions flush.

Cut and fit the axle spacers. Clamp the spacers against the axle. The T1-11 is absorbent, so use plenty of glue and lots of screws.

Cap the frame. Fit cap pieces onto the top edge of the cart and screw them in place. They'll get dinged up in use, and eventually you'll need to replace them, so don't glue them.

side, and screw them to the T1-11 from inside the cart. Use the 1⅝-inch galvanized screws.

9 Cut and fit the axle spacers. The spacers, which are sawn from scraps of T1-11, trap the axle in place. Fit the wheels on the axle in order to locate the washers and nuts, then remove the wheels. Set the axle into the little valley between the two support blocks. Spread glue on one of the spacers, then fit it tightly against the axle. Drill pilot holes and screw the spacers to the axle support blocks and bottom frame. Spread glue on the second spacer, clamp it tight against the axle, and screw it down in the same way.

10 Cap the axle. The axle retainer, which is another strip of T1-11, caps the axle assembly. This strip has to be strong, so when you saw it from the plywood sheet, avoid the decorative grooves. Spread the glue

and drill pilot holes for 24 of the 2½-inch screws. Drill the pilot holes and drive the screws at various angles, which will strengthen the construction. You may hit a screw in the next layer down. If so, back out the one you were driving, and move it over a half inch or so.

11 Mount the wheels. Slide a washer onto the threaded rod, then a nut, then another washer, then the wheel, then another washer, then two nuts jammed tight together. The first nut and washer keep the tire from rubbing the cart sides.

12 Complete the frame. Reinforce the top of the T1-11 cart body with four frame pieces. These pieces fit on the outside of the T1-11, flush with its top edge. They'll be capped with four more pieces of wood in the next step. The top end frames are pieces of 2×4 sawn in half lengthwise and then cut to

fit between the end frames. The top side frames are 1×2 strips of pine. Glue, clamp, and screw these frame pieces onto the cart. Then trim any protruding pieces flush with their mates, as shown in the top right photo.

13 Cap the frame. Four strips of 1×3 wood cap the cart sides, covering the joints between the T1-11 and the frame pieces. The cap pieces are certain to get banged up, so consider them replaceable parts. Screw them down, but skip the glue.

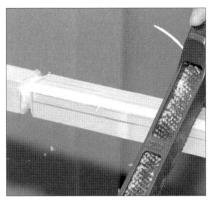
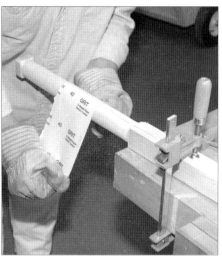

Make the handles. Draw layout lines and use a coarse round file or Surform to make a groove at both ends of the handle section (above left). Rasp off the corners of the handle to make an octagon, then rasp off the octagon's corners (center). This brings you close to round. Sand the handle with 40-grit paper, then move through 80-grit and 120-grit (right).

14 Make the handles. Saw a 5-foot-long 2×4 in half lengthwise to make two handle blanks. Choose knot-free wood with closely spaced annual rings. Shape the 15-inch rounded sections with Surform rasps and sandpaper, as shown in the photos above.

15 Fit the handles. Clamp one handle to the cart and test it. Adjust the angle so the lift is comfortable for you. Draw a layout line, and transfer the layout line to the other side of the cart. Unclamp the handles, drill pilot holes through the cart sides, and countersink the pilot holes on the inside of the cart. Glue and screw the handles to the cart sides. Drive at least six 2-inch screws into each handle.

16 Make the legs. The legs, which are pieces of 2×4, should prop the cart up level. The top of the leg fits against the handle. Hold the 2×4 in place so you can lay out the angle on the bottom of the legs, as shown at right. Saw the legs to length, then glue and screw them in place.

Fit the handles. Clamp one handle to the cart sides so you can check the lift. Adjust the handle to your own height.

17 Finish the cart. You could leave the cart unfinished, or you could paint it. The traditional finish for working tools is boiled linseed oil. Let the oil soak into the wood, then wipe it off with a rag. Let it dry for a week, then coat it again. If you wad up an oily rag, it's liable to ignite spontaneously, so spread the rag outdoors to dry flat. When it's completely dry and stiff, put it in the trash.

Make the legs. The leg fits square against the handle, so it needs to be sawn on an angle at the ground. Hold it in place, then draw a layout line against a block of wood.

COLD FRAME

Wooden box with glass lid protects tender plants from cold winds

A cold frame is a little greenhouse without heat. It gives the gardener an early start in the spring, and a place to shelter tender plants that can't handle the local winter. The cold frame sits directly on the ground. The loose-fitting glass lid can be lifted and propped up for ventilation on sunny days, or it can be slid to one side. An additional ventilation slot in the back of the box can be left open, or covered with a slat of wood.

You've probably seen published designs for large cold frames with elaborate and even automated lid-lifting mechanisms. However, cold frames in established gardens are more likely to be wondrous old things tacked together from salvaged storm windows and peeling wood. They're utility construc-

tions, not works of art or pieces of furniture. It's OK to make them in a rustic manner.

Grandiose frames actually don't function as well as a small cold frame, like the one shown here. It's easy to work with and to move. You can reach from one side to the other, without having to walk all around. When you need more acreage under glass, simply build more frames.

COLD FRAME

Screw the box fronts and sides together, then screw the sloping side to the box. Trim the ends flush. Make the glass frame from the inside out: Join inner frame rails to inner frame stiles, attach muntins and glazing strips, attach the outer frame to the inner frame.

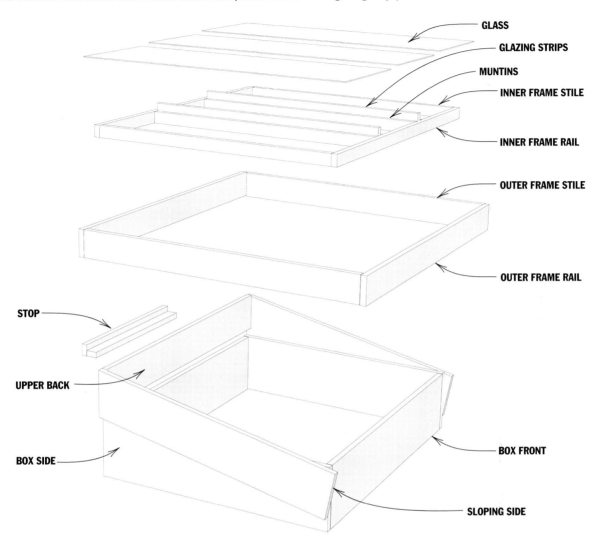

YOUR INVESTMENT

<u>Time:</u> One afternoon
<u>Money:</u> $25 for wood, $12 for glass

SHOPPING LIST

12 feet 1×8 roughsawn pine
10 feet 1×6 roughsawn pine
24 feet 1×2 pine
6 feet 1×3 pine
16 feet 1×4 pine
#6 × 1½-inch galvanized screws
#6 × 2-inch galvanized screws
#8 × 2½-inch galvanized screws
9 square feet double-strength window glass

PROJECT SPECS

The cold frame measures 42 inches wide, 40 inches front to back, and 17 inches high.

CUTTING LIST

PART	QTY.	DIMENSIONS	NOTES
Box side	2	$\frac{3}{4} \times 8 \times 32$	
Box front	2	$\frac{3}{4} \times 8 \times 36$	
Sloping side	2	$\frac{3}{4} \times 6 \times 34$	Trim ends
Upper back	1	$\frac{3}{4} \times 5 \times 38$	Trim to fit
Inner frame rail	2	$\frac{3}{4} \times 1\frac{1}{2} \times 40\frac{1}{2}$	1×2
Inner frame stile	2	$\frac{3}{4} \times 1\frac{1}{2} \times 32\frac{1}{4}$	1×2
Muntin	2	$\frac{3}{4} \times 2\frac{1}{2} \times 32\frac{1}{4}$	1×3
Glazing strip	4	$\frac{3}{4} \times 1\frac{1}{2} \times 32\frac{1}{4}$	1×2
Outer frame stile	2	$\frac{3}{4} \times 3\frac{1}{2} \times 38$	1×4
Outer frame rail	2	$\frac{3}{4} \times 3\frac{1}{2} \times 42$	1×4
Stop	2	$\frac{3}{4} \times 1\frac{1}{2} \times 19$	
Glass	3	$\frac{3}{8} \times 13 \times 35$	

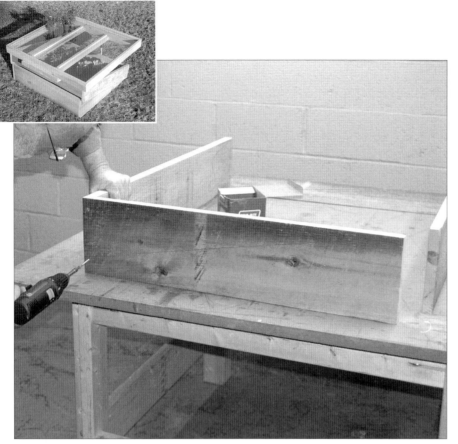

Make the box. Screw through the face of the box sides into the end grain of the box front and back.

Attach the sloping sides. Position the sloping side 1¾ inches up from the bottom front corner, and crossing the top back corner (left). Clamp the sloping side in place and screw it to the box side (above).

BUILDING THE COLD FRAME

1 Cut all the wood. The box in the photos is made with ¼ rough-sawn pine lumber, which is cheap and plentiful in our part of New England. You can use the rough lumber that grows in your region, or whatever salvaged wood you might have around, or regular pine boards from the home center. The frame, which holds the glass, can also be made of salvaged material or of smooth pine lumber. Cut all the wood to length at the start of the project, though the upper back piece will have to be trimmed to fit in Step 5.

2 Make the box. Screw the box sides to the box front and back with three of the 2½-inch screws in each corner, as shown in the photo at top left. The screws go through the face of the sides, which are the shorter pieces, into the end grain of the front and back.

3 Attach the sloping sides. The slope allows the cold frame to catch the winter sunlight and to shed rain and snow, but the amount of slope is quite arbitrary. As shown in the photos at left, the slope arises from the way the sloping sides are positioned on the box sides: 1¾ inches up from the bottom front corner, and smack on the top back corner. Fasten the sloping sides from inside the box, using four 1½-inch screws.

4 Trim the ends. The back end of the sloping sides has to be brought into line with the end of the main box. Use a straightedge or a framing square to extend

Trim the ends. Extend the line of the box across the back end of the sloping side (left). Jigsaw the sloping side flush with the box back (above).

the line of the box across the wood, and saw it on the line. Use a jigsaw, as shown in the photos above, or a handsaw.

5 **Make the upper back.** The width of the upper back piece is somewhat arbitrary. It should be less than the rise of the sloping sides, in order to leave a slot for ventilation. How much less depends on what the gardener intends to do with the cold frame, as well as on the available wood. The upper back can be made of two narrow slats of wood, if you prefer. Drive screws through the sloping sides into the end grain of the upper back.

6 **Make the inner glass frame.** The glass frame is a two-layer construction, both for strength and in order to create a rabbet for the glass itself. Begin by making the inner frame, which consists of two rails and two stiles. The longer rails overlap the ends of the stiles, as shown in the photo at right. Hold the first corner together on the worktable and drive two screws through the face of the rail and into the end grain of the stile.

Make the upper back. Fit the upper back between the two sloping sides and screw it in position. The gap ventilates the cold frame.

Make the inner glass frame. Clamp the rails and stiles of the inner glass frame to the worktable, and screw them together. The rails, which are longer than the stiles, overlap the ends of the stiles.

Join the other four corners in the same way.

7 Fit the muntins. The two muntins are the same length as the inner frame stiles in Step 6, but they are an inch wider. This extra width will create the glass rabbets in the center of the frame. Divide the width of the frame in thirds to locate the muntins. Screw through the inner frame rails into the ends of the muntins with the 2-inch screws, as shown below.

8 Make the glazing strips. The four glazing strips are screwed to either side of the center stiles, forming the glass rabbet. Fit the glazing strips in place and clamp them to the stiles.

Screw them to the inner frame rails, and to the center stiles, as shown in the photos at the bottom of the page.

9 Attach the outer frame stiles. The outer frame stiles continue the glass rabbets and form the lip that keeps the glass frame on the box. The outer frame stiles fit flush with the inner frame stiles at one end, with a 4-inch overhang at the other, which will become the front. Center the inner frame on the width of the outer frame rails, as shown in the photo at the top of the facing page, and screw the parts together from the inside, using $1\frac{1}{4}$-inch screws.

10 Make the outer frame rails. The outer frame rails complete the glass frame. They're screwed to the end grain of the outer frame stiles, as shown in the photos in the center of the facing page. Also screw the rear rail to the inner frame stile.

11 Make the lid stop. The lid stop keeps the lid from skidding

Fit the muntins. Divide the width of the inner frame into thirds and fit the muntins. Screw through the rails into the end grain of the muntins.

Make the glazing strips. Screw a glazing strip to each side of the muntins (above). Drive a screw through the inner frame rails into the ends of the muntins as well (left).

off the frame when it's propped open. It consists of two pieces of 1×2 pine screwed together to the back of the box, as shown in the bottom left photo.

12 Glaze the cold frame. When you buy glass, specify panes ¼ inch narrower than the openings in the cold frame, and a full inch shorter. This gap allows the glass to drain. Set the glass in its rabbets, and secure it with a few glazing points. Press the points into the wood with a putty knife, as shown at bottom right.

Attach the outer frame stiles. Center the outer frame stiles on the inner frame, with a 4-inch overhang toward the front (left in the photo above).

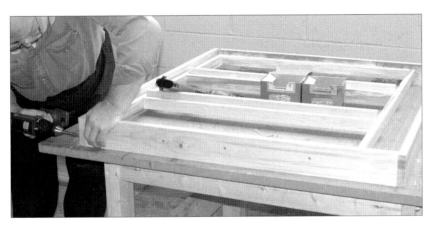

Make the outer frame rails. Screw the outer frame rails to the inner frame (left) and to the ends of the outer frame stiles (above).

Make the lid stop. Screw two pieces of 1×2 to the back of the box, to make a lid stop (above).

Glaze the cold frame. Set the glass in its rabbets and anchor it with glazing points (right).

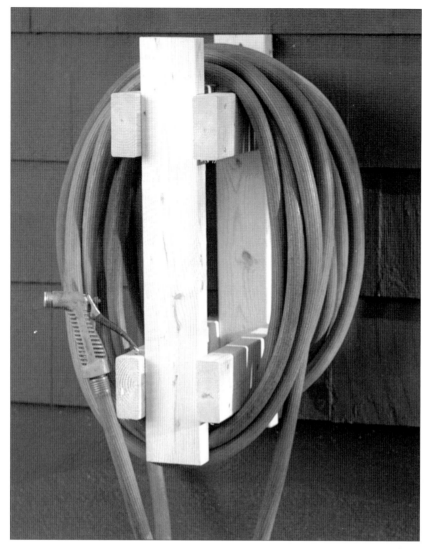

Spike the arms onto the uprights. Nail both arms flush with the edge of one upright (above). Drive the nails at an angle to one another, for maximum holding power. Nail the second upright to the free ends of the arms, inset by the thickness of a piece of scrap (below). Fasten the second set of arms to the other side of the uprights (bottom).

HOSE HOLDER

Simple device gets the hose off the ground without tangles

Garden hoses get into a terrible tangle if they're not kept coiled. The devices that the home center sells are lightweight contraptions, when what's needed is something sturdy and substantial, like the hose holder shown here.

This hose holder can be made in either of two variations,

a small one that can be fastened to the side of the house, and a larger one that can be staked to the ground. If your house has wooden siding, you probably wouldn't object to screwing the hose holder directly onto it. However, if your house has aluminum or vinyl siding, you may prefer the staked version.

BUILDING THE WALL HOLDER

1 Cut the wood. Make the hose holder parts from regular 2×4 lumber, or from scraps of 2×4 left over from other projects.

2 Spike the arms onto the uprights. The arms are flush with the upright that's going to be fastened to the wall, but they extend an inch beyond the other upright. The uprights extend above and below the arms by $3\frac{1}{2}$ inches. Make layout lines and attach two arms to the same edge of one upright, using three 3-inch spiral nails at each intersection. Nail the second upright to the free ends of the arms, as shown in the photos at left. Then turn the assembly over to add the other two arms.

3 Mount the holder on the wall. Drill clearance holes for six 3-inch screws, two at the top, two at the bottom and two at center. Screw the upright to the side of the house or garage near the water spigot, as shown below. Loop the hose loosely over the hose holder, as shown in the opening photo.

Mount the holder on the wall. Screw the hose holder to the wall near the water spigot. Screw into a wall stud.

WALL-MOUNTED HOSE HOLDER

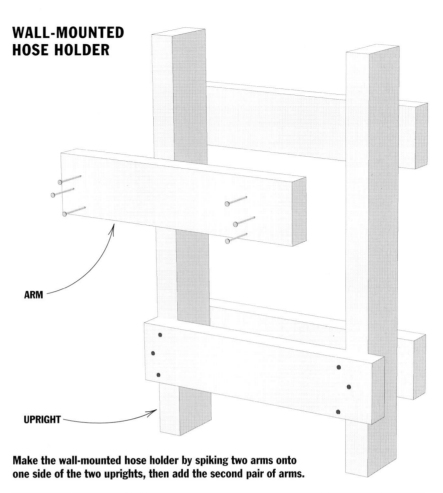

ARM

UPRIGHT

Make the wall-mounted hose holder by spiking two arms onto one side of the two uprights, then add the second pair of arms.

YOUR INVESTMENT
Time: One hour
Money: Wall-mounted hose holder, $5; staked hose holder, $25

SHOPPING LIST
Wall-mounted hose holder
10 feet 2×4
Staked hose holder
4 feet 4×4
8 feet 2×3
4 feet 2×4
24-inch metal stake for 4×4 post
3-inch galvanized spiral nails

PROJECT SPECS
The wall-mounted hose holder is 24 inches high and projects 16 inches from the wall. The staked hose holder stands 42 inches high and is 24 inches wide.

CUTTING LIST

PART	QTY.	DIMENSIONS	NOTES
Wall-mounted hose holder			
Upright	2	$1\frac{1}{2} \times 3\frac{1}{2} \times 24$	2×4
Arm	4	$1\frac{1}{2} \times 3\frac{1}{2} \times 16$	2×4
Staked hose holder			
Post	1	$3\frac{1}{2} \times 3\frac{1}{2} \times 42$	4×4
Upright	2	$1\frac{1}{2} \times 3\frac{1}{2} \times 24$	2×4
Arm	4	$1\frac{1}{2} \times 2\frac{1}{2} \times 24$	2×3

Cut the wood. Instead of a 4×4 post, you can bulk up a pair of 2×4s with a ¹/₂-inch center insert of solid wood or scrap plywood.

Attach the arms. Nail the arms to the post with 3-inch spiral nails. Drive the first nail and start the second, then check for square.

Attach the uprights. Fit the uprights between the arms and nail them in place.

STAKED HOSE HOLDER

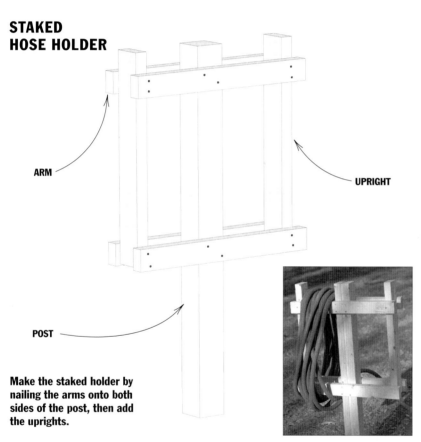

ARM

UPRIGHT

POST

Make the staked holder by nailing the arms onto both sides of the post, then add the uprights.

BUILDING THE STAKED HOLDER

1 Cut the wood. Unless you are willing to use pressure treated lumber, you may have difficulty obtaining a 4×4 post. However, you can assemble the post from two lengths of regular 2×4, with a center insert to bring it up to the thickness that fits the cup atop a commercially made metal stake, as shown at top left. Make the center insert from a scrap strip of ¹/₂-inch plywood, or by sawing two ¹/₂-inch strips from the edge of a third piece of 2×4.

2 Attach the arms. The 2×3 arms are centered on the face of the post. The upper arms are set down by 3½ inches from the top of the post. The lower arms are set flush with the bottom of the uprights. Attach each arm to the post with two 3-inch spiral nails. Hold the arm in position to drive the first nail and to start the second, then pause and check it for square before driving the second nail home, as shown in the photo at center above. Turn the post over to attach the second set of arms in the same way as the first.

3 Attach the uprights. Fit the uprights between the arms. Make each upright flush with the bottom edge of the lower arms, but inset by about an inch. Fasten the upright to the arms with two 3-inch spiral nails at each intersection, as shown in the top right photo.

4 Drive the stake and set the post. Decide where you want to install the hose holder and drive the stake into the ground, same as for the garden fence on page 68. Connect the hose to your faucet and spray away.

BEAN TEEPEE

Eight climbing poles make a comfy home for French beans

French beans run all over the place, unless you give them a teepee to climb. Then they're perfectly happy and you will be too, because the harvest stays within easy bounds.

This bean teepee consists of a wood-and-nails spider attached to eight 1×2 climbing poles. You can set it wherever you like, then fold it up like an umbrella at the end of the season.

BUILDING THE TEEPEE

1 Cut the wood. The cutting list specifies 1×2 material for the climbing poles, but you can use any wood you've got: narrow rippings, gardening stakes, what-ever. They don't have to all match, and they don't bear any appreciable weight, so knots and defects are not important.

2 Make the spider. The spider is a square block of wood with eight nails coming out of it. Choose a straight-grained scrap of wood, so it's less likely to

BEAN TEEPEE

SPIDER

CLIMBING POLE

NAIL

Drive eight nails into a block of wood to make the spider. Drill holes in the eight climbing poles and thread them onto the nails.

YOUR INVESTMENT
Time: One hour
Money: $5

PROJECT SPECS
The bean teepee stands 7 feet high and spreads about 5 feet.

SHOPPING LIST
56 feet 1×2 pine
2½ inch spiral nails

CUTTING LIST

PART	QTY.	DIMENSIONS	NOTES
Spider	1	$\frac{3}{4} \times 4\frac{1}{2} \times 4\frac{1}{2}$	
Climbing pole	8	$\frac{3}{4} \times 1\frac{1}{2} \times 84$	

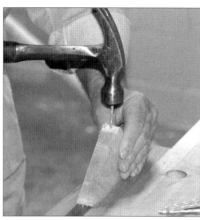

Make the spider. Mash a flat on the corner of a square block of wood (left). Drive nails into the corners and the centers of the sides (right).

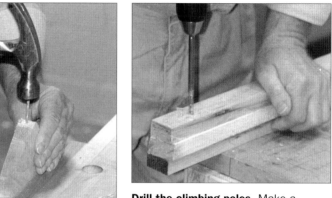

Drill the climbing poles. Make a $\frac{5}{16}$-inch hole near the end of each of the eight climbing poles. Drill the poles in groups of two or three.

Erect the teepee. Thread the climbing poles onto the spider (above). Spread the poles and bed them into the ground. Then plant the beans (right).

split. Hold the wood in a vise if you have one, or else balance it on the worktable. To make a nailing flat at the corner of the spider, mash the wood with the hammer. Drive a 2½-inch spiral nail into the center of each edge, and into each corner, as shown in the top left photos.

3 Drill the climbing poles. Drill a $\frac{5}{16}$-inch hole a couple of inches from the end of each climbing pole. Drill the poles two or three at a time, as shown in the top right photo.

4 Erect the teepee. Slip the climbing poles onto the spider nails. Spread the poles as far apart as the nails permit and push them into the soil.

RASPBERRY POST

Supports put the canes on a manageable path

RASPBERRY POST

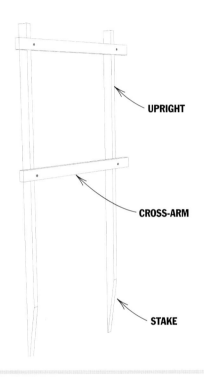

- UPRIGHT
- CROSS-ARM
- STAKE

YOUR INVESTMENT

Time: One hour
Money: $4

SHOPPING LIST

13 feet 1×2
#6 × 2-inch galvanized screws
Gardening twine

PROJECT SPECS

One raspberry post is 48 inches high and 24 inches wide.

CUTTING LIST

PART	QTY.	DIMENSIONS	NOTES
Upright	2	$3/4 \times 1\frac{1}{2} \times 48$	
Cross-arm	2	$3/4 \times 1\frac{1}{2} \times 24$	

Saw the point on the uprights, then screw the cross-arms to them. Install the raspberry posts, then tie twine between the cross-arms to support the raspberry canes.

Sharpen the uprights and stakes.
Draw a diagonal line starting from the corner of the stake, and jigsaw a point.

Join the uprights and cross-arms.
Screw the uprights to the edges of the cross-arms.

Raspberries make a brambly mess if left to themselves, but unlike beans, they prefer to grow along a horizontal line instead of up a vertical pole. These simple trellises also work for peas and sweetpeas. Make raspberry posts in pairs, one for either end of the row, and connect them with twine, not wire.

BUILDING THE POSTS

1 Cut the wood. You can get one raspberry post out of an 8-foot 1×2, but you can also use scrap wood or garden stakes.

2 Sharpen the uprights. Sharpen the uprights to make it easy to set the raspberry post a few inches into the ground. Draw a diagonal line off one corner of the upright to a point 9 inches up, and jigsaw the point as shown in the top photo.

3 Join the uprights and cross-arms. A single screw makes an adequate connection between each upright and cross-arm. Screw through the face of the cross arm into the edge of the upright. Space the cross-arms about 16 inches apart.

4 Install the raspberry post. Set the raspberry posts in early spring, just as last year's canes begin to sprout new runners. Shove them 6 or 8 inches into the soil. Connect the cross-arms with lengths of twine, at least two and as many as four between each pair of cross-arms. Finally, run diagonal lengths of twine from the top cross-arm back to a 12-inch stake driven into the ground. This not only stabilizes the posts, it also makes an additional line for the raspberry runners to climb.

BOOT SCRAPER

Leave the mud in the garden, not inside the house

Woe betide the gardener who tracks great clots of spring muck into the clean house. But what is the hapless peasant to do, without a premier boot scraper like the one shown here? This sturdy beast, which you should set up near the gar-

den hose, allows you to scrape and brush the muck out of the deepest foot-treads. It's even got a place to lean while you shuck your gumboots and change into dry sneakers. And the duckboard construction makes it a snap to hose clean.

No doubt you could design a smaller and lighter version of the boot scraper. But if you're serious about gardening, then you'll have a serious amount of muck to contend with. You need to kick and bang and stomp on an apparatus built to take it. Likewise, if you enjoy whaling away with your framing hammer, you could knock this scraper together with spiral nails. Otherwise, clamp the pieces and drive galvanized screws, as discussed below.

BUILDING THE BOOT SCRAPER

1 Cut all the wood. You're going to screw the duckboard slats to one rail and then to the other, so it's important to make all the slats the same length. Guarantee equal lengths by setting a stop block on your table saw or chop saw.

2 Start the duckboard. There are two rails and eleven slats in the duckboard. Clamp the first slat to the worktable and butt the first rail up to it. Drill clearance holes and join the two pieces with two of the 3-inch screws. Then insert a couple of scraps of 2×4 as spacers, and screw the next slat to the rail, as shown in the top left photo on page 48. Continue in the same way until you have attached five slats to the first rail.

BOOT SCRAPER

Screw the duckboard rails and slats together. Add the posts and scraping bar, then the brush posts and brush bar. Screw the brushes to the slats and brush bar. Add the handrail.

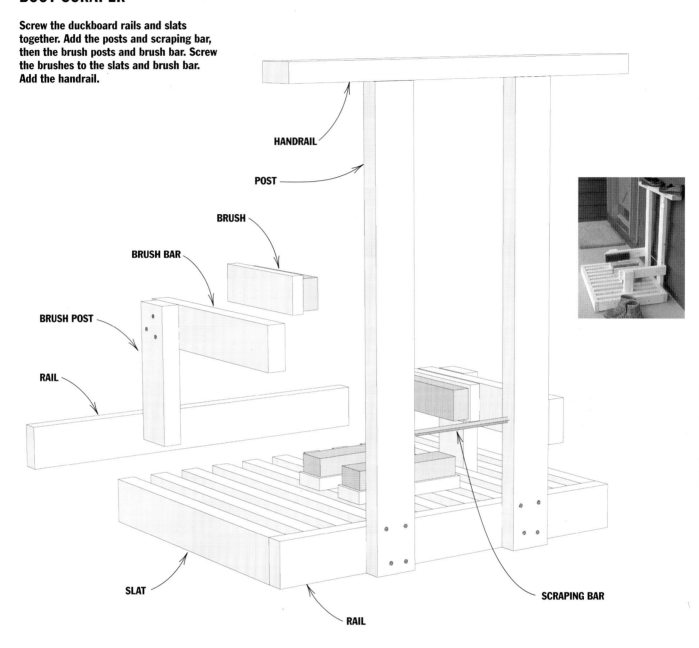

HANDRAIL

POST

BRUSH

BRUSH BAR

BRUSH POST

RAIL

SLAT

RAIL

SCRAPING BAR

YOUR INVESTMENT

<u>Time:</u> One afternoon
<u>Money:</u> $30

SHOPPING LIST

Six 8-foot 2×4
$^5/_{16} \times {}^5/_{16} \times$ **12-inch square
steel bar**
**Four 10-inch scrub brushes with
wooden handles**
#8 × 3-inch galvanized screws
#6 × 2-inch galvanized screws

PROJECT SPECS

The boot scraper is 32 inches wide, 36 inches high and 30 inches front to back.

CUTTING LIST

PART	QTY.	DIMENSIONS	NOTES
Slat	11	$1^1/_2 \times 3^1/_2 \times 24$	2×4
Rail	2	$1^1/_2 \times 3^1/_2 \times 32$	2×4
Post	2	$1^1/_2 \times 3^1/_2 \times 36$	2×4
Brush post	2	$1^1/_2 \times 3^1/_2 \times 11$	2×4
Brush bar	2	$1^1/_2 \times 3^1/_2 \times 18$	2×4
Handrail	1	$1^1/_2 \times 3^1/_2 \times 32$	2×4
Scraping bar	1	$^5/_{16} \times {}^5/_{16} \times 12$	Steel

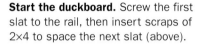

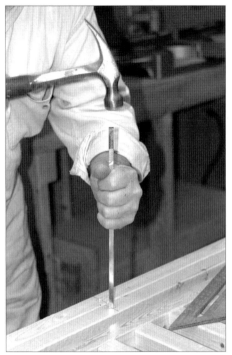

Start the duckboard. Screw the first slat to the rail, then insert scraps of 2×4 to space the next slat (above).

Complete the duckboard. Work from the ends toward the middle, so any uneven spacing turns up between the middle two slats. Then screw the second rail to the free end of the slats (top right).

Mount the scraping bar. Drill a $^5/_{16}$-inch hole for the scraping bar in each post, then hammer the bar into one of the holes (left). Make sure to turn the bar corner up. Remove the bar and hammer it into the other post, then fit the two posts together (right).

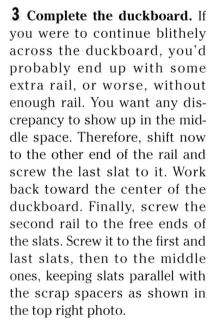

Screw the posts to the duckboard. Clamp the posts to the rails and make them parallel. Adjust their spacing so that the outside edge of each post lines up with the inside edge of a slat.

3 Complete the duckboard. If you were to continue blithely across the duckboard, you'd probably end up with some extra rail, or worse, without enough rail. You want any discrepancy to show up in the middle space. Therefore, shift now to the other end of the rail and screw the last slat to it. Work back toward the center of the duckboard. Finally, screw the second rail to the free ends of the slats. Screw it to the first and last slats, then to the middle ones, keeping slats parallel with the scrap spacers as shown in the top right photo.

4 Mount the scraping bar. The boot scraping bar is a square rod of steel trapped between the two posts. It's 10 inches up from

the bottom of the posts, centered on their edges. Lay out and drill a $^5/_{16}$-inch hole about $1^1/_4$-inch deep in the edge of each post. Hold the steel rod corner up, and hammer it an inch into one post, as shown in the center left photo. Wiggle the rod out of the hole, and hammer it about an inch into the other post. Then put the first post back in position and tap it onto the rod, as shown in the photo above.

5 Screw the posts to the duck-board. Center the posts-and-bar assembly on one rail of the duckboard. The outside edge of each post should line up with the inside edge of a slat, as shown in the lower left photo. Align and square one post and drive four screws into the duck-

Attach the sole brushes. Drill pilot holes and screw the two sole brushes to the duckboards.

Mount the brush posts. Locate the brush posts between the slats and screw them to the slats.

Attach the brush bars. Clamp the brush bars in position and screw them to the posts and to the brush posts.

Attach the side brushes. Screw the side brushes to the brush bars. Let them extend an inch or so beyond the ends of the bars.

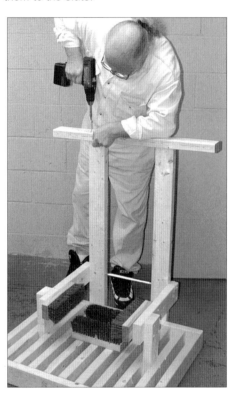

Make the handrail. Screw the handrail to the ends of the posts.

board rail. Then hammer the other post a little further onto the bar, or a little bit off the bar, until it too aligns with the inside edge of a slat, and screw it to the rail in the same way.

6 Attach the sole brushes. Screw the two boot-sole brushes directly to the duckboard slats, centered between the posts. Leave clearance of about 6 inches to the posts, and 3 inches between the brushes, as shown in the photo at top left. Drill clearance holes through the brush backs and fasten them to the slats with 2-inch screws.

7 Mount the brush posts. The two vertical brush posts support the brush bars. Mount them in the second space from

either side of the duckboard, 12 inches from the outside of the back rail. This measurement creates an offset of 1½ inches between the brush post and the end of the brush bar. Screw diagonally down through the duckboard slats into the face of the brush posts, as shown in the photo at top right.

8 Attach the brush bars. The two horizontal brush bars support the brushes that allow you to grind the muck off the sides of your boots. Screw them to the posts and to the brush posts, as shown in the lower left photo.

9 Attach the side brushes. Clamp the side brushes to the brush bars. Keep the brush flush with the top of the bar, but let it

overhang 1½ inches toward the front. Drill clearance holes through the brush bars into the backs of the two side brushes. Screw the brushes to the brush bars, as shown in center photo.

10 Make the handrail. The handrail is a horizontal 2×4 screwed to the tops of the posts. Center it and fasten it with two 3-inch screws into each post, as shown above.

COMPOST BOX

Sturdy frame opens on one side

Seasoned gardeners develop their own approaches to composting, and their own box designs, but this simple box is a good way to get started. It has slatted sides and ends, so the air can circulate, and the front of the box lifts out, so you can turn the pile. When it's time to move the composted material into the garden, tip the box over and shovel the black gold.

The box shown is big enough for a household's kitchen and garden waste, plus the autumn leaves from a couple of trees. You can refigure the box to any size you like, and if you make several of them, you'll have enough microbial spas to decompose the largest garden.

You could make the compost box with regular pine lumber from the home center. But it is a compost box, not a piece of furniture, so it's the perfect place for using up scrap wood and short ends. The box shown takes advantage of a pile of mangy, roughsawn pine boards that had sat out in the weather. Your scrap material will be different from ours, so you'll have to work out the number of pieces from the widths you have. Just be sure to leave one-inch spaces for air to circulate, and avoid painted wood and pressure-treated lumber.

Ultimately, of course, the compost box goes the way of all organic material. By then, you will have formed your own opinion about how compost should be managed. You will be equipped by experience to design your own compost box.

BUILDING THE COMPOST BOX

1 **Make the corner posts and flanges.** Saw the four 2×3 corner posts to their final length, 36 inches in the box shown here. Make the four flanges the same length as the corner posts.

2 **Nail the front posts.** The flange pieces are nailed to the front corner posts, to make them into U-shaped channels. Align each flange piece with the ends and one edge of the corner post, then attach it with five or six 2½-inch spiral nails, as shown at top left on the next page. Attach two flange pieces to each front corner post.

COMPOST BOX

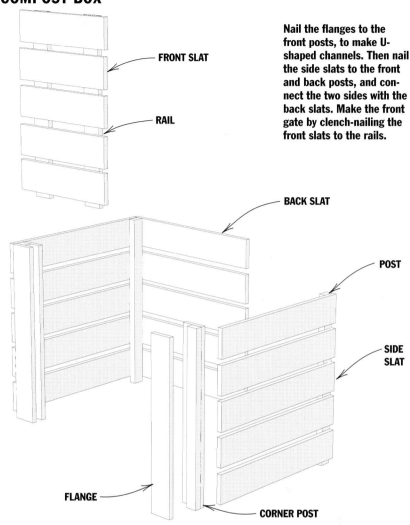

FRONT SLAT

RAIL

Nail the flanges to the front posts, to make U-shaped channels. Then nail the side slats to the front and back posts, and connect the two sides with the back slats. Make the front gate by clench-nailing the front slats to the rails.

BACK SLAT

POST

SIDE SLAT

FLANGE

CORNER POST

YOUR INVESTMENT
<u>Time:</u> **One afternoon**
<u>Money:</u> **$25**

SHOPPING LIST
12 feet 2×3 pine
18 feet 1×5 roughsawn pine
54 feet 1×6 roughsawn pine
2 ½-inch galvanized spiral nails
3-inch galvanized spiral nails

PROJECT SPECS
The compost box is 33 inches wide, 37 inches deep and 36 inches high.

CUTTING LIST

PART	QTY.	DIMENSIONS	NOTES
Corner post	4	1 ½ × 2 ½ × 36	2×3
Flange	4	1 × 5 × 36	
Side slat	10	1 × 6 × 36	
Back slat	5	1 × 6 × 33	
Front slat	5	1 × 6 × 24	
Rail	2	1 × 4 × 36	

Nail the front posts. Make U-shaped channels by nailing two flange pieces to each front post, using spiral nails (above). Align the pieces on the back side (below).

Nail the side slats to the front posts. Make the side panels by nailing the side slats to the closed side of the U-shaped channel formed by the front posts and flanges.

3 **Nail the side slats to the front posts.** The side slats of the compost box are 36-inch lengths of ¾-inch or 1-inch thick wood, between 4 and 6 inches wide. Starting at the top of one front post, nail each slat to the post as shown in the photo at bottom left. Drive four of the 2½-inch spiral nails into each intersection. Use a length of regular 1×2 lumber to space the slats. Organize the side slats so that when you get to the bottom of the post, there's a space of 2 inches to 4 inches in width. Nail the second set of side slats to the other front post in the same way, but take care to make a right side and a left side.

4 **Nail the side slats to the rear posts.** Since the rear post is a regular 2×3, you'll have to drape the front flanges over the edge of the worktable, as shown in the photos below. Nail the free ends of the side slats to each rear post. You should end up with two similar side panels, one right-handed and the other left-handed.

5 **Nail the back slats to the sides.** Stand the two completed side panels up on end, with the flanged front posts on the ground. Space the back slats across the sides. Connect the two sides by squaring and fastening the top back slat in place,

Nail the side slats to the rear posts. Align the free ends of the side slats with the rear post (above). Nail them together (below).

using the 3-inch spiral nails. Nail the bottom back slat, then fill in the space with the remaining slats. Spiral nails are stiff enough, and the nailing surfaces are wide enough, for the box to stand on its own without any bracing across the open front side.

6 Make the front panel. The front slats are clench-nailed to two rails, as discussed in the box below. Make sure the front slats will fit into the U-channeled front posts with ½-inch clearance. Then set the rails far enough in from the ends of the slats so they don't interfere—1¾ inches to 2 inches is about right. Align the top slat with the end of the first rail and drive the first nail. Then check for square, and drive the remaining three nails. Attach the top slat to the other rail in the same way, measuring to be sure the rails remain parallel to one another. Fasten the bottom slat, then fill in with the remaining front slats. Clench all the nails on the back of the panel to ensure that the construction stays together until the wood itself rots.

Nail the back slats to the sides. Stand the two side panels up on end and connect them with the back slats.

Make the front panel. Fasten the front slats to the rails with four nails at each intersection. Drive the nails on an angle and clench them on the back side, as discussed below.

CLENCH-NAILING

Clench-nailing means driving the points of the nails clear through the wood and bending them over on the back side. It is a certain way of holding nailed constructions together. Wooden pallets and stage sets are clench-nailed, and so are farm buildings throughout the Midwest. It's said that a clench-nailed shed can be picked up by a tornado and set down intact.

For a good clench, the nail should protrude about ½ inch on the back side of the wood. Drive the nails at a small angle, say 10 degrees from vertical. Then turn the work over and bend the points down hard into the wood. Do it right, and the nail head won't lift on the front side. Do it with less than full vigor, and the nail head probably will lift, making a secure but wiggly joint.

Clench-nailing. Drive the nails through the two pieces of wood, then bend the protruding points down tight.

GREENHOUSE CABINET

Extend the growing season with this rollaway glass box

Every gardener dreams of a greenhouse, but few can manage the expenditure of space or money. However, you can extend your growing season on a small scale with this handsome greenhouse cabinet. It offers you most of the virtues of a full-size greenhouse, without all of the expense. It's small enough to park on the corner of your condo deck, backyard patio or apartment balcony. You can roll it around to capture the best light, and it rolls away for the off-season.

The greenhouse cabinet has small panes, so you can use ordinary single-strength glass. Complete the cabinet, and measure the actual openings, before you order the glass. Make sure there's ⅛ inch of clearance, so the glass can expand and contract with temperature changes. You could save money by stapling polyethylene to the framework instead of using glass.

The back is made of ⅜-inch exterior-grade plywood. The bottom uses up the remains of the plywood sheet, screwed to a sturdy 2×4 base. The heavy base permits the cabinet to roll across an uneven deck without flexing, thereby protecting the glass from breaking.

The greenhouse cabinet features a hinged top, which can be propped open at any height for more or less ventilation. The

The greenhouse cabinet features sliding shelves made of wire mesh or hardware cloth, so the light will filter through to the plants below.

shelves, made of wire mesh, slide easily through the double-door opening. You can load a shelf with seedlings, slide it out to work on the plants, then slide it back into the cabinet.

The cabinet sides, doors and skylights are made of ordinary 1×2 pine lumber, which actually measures ¾ inch thick and 1½ inches wide. However, it's important to avoid large knots. Small, tight knots will not cause a problem, but large knots with black edges of bark are liable to fall out, weakening the structure. No. 2 pine will do if you can choose your wood at the home center. If you can't choose, consider paying extra for "select" or "clear" wood.

This is a large project with a lot of pieces of wood, and accu-racy is important. However, the construction is straightforward and modular, and you can complete each assembly before moving on to the next. The key skill you need is the ability to saw a stick of wood square and to length. You will need to miter the ends of a few of the 1×2s at 12½ degrees, and you can save money by sawing your own glazing strips, as discussed in Step 1 on page 58.

Except for a coat of white paint on the plywood back and bottom, we left our cabinet unfinished. If you want to finish yours, the right material is paint, but you must make the decision before you install the glass. That way you can paint the wood without struggling to keep paint off the glass.

GREENHOUSE CABINET

The greenhouse cabinet looks complex but its construction is simple and modular. Make the base and back, then the two sides, then the doors and skylight, and finally the shelves.

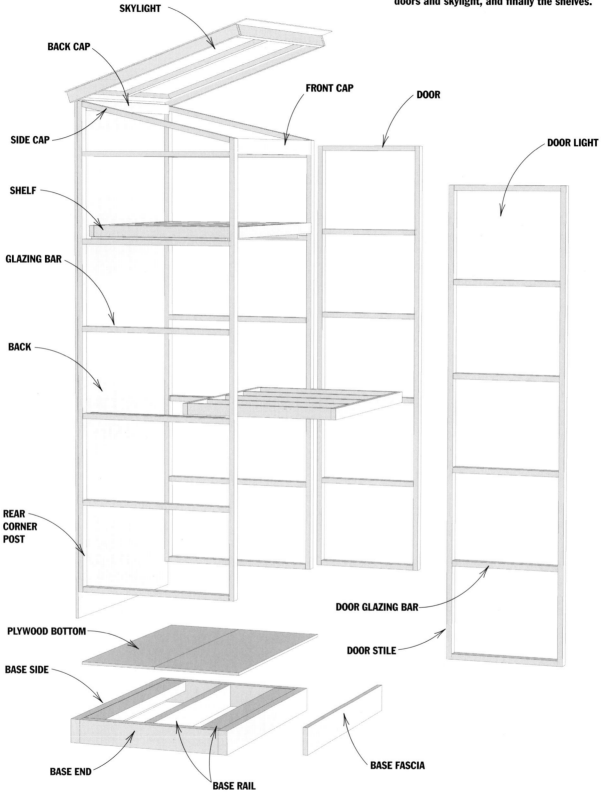

SKYLIGHT

BACK CAP

FRONT CAP

DOOR

DOOR LIGHT

SIDE CAP

SHELF

GLAZING BAR

BACK

REAR CORNER POST

DOOR GLAZING BAR

DOOR STILE

PLYWOOD BOTTOM

BASE SIDE

BASE END

BASE RAIL

BASE FASCIA

YOUR INVESTMENT

<u>Time:</u> One weekend
<u>Money:</u> Glass and acrylic, $85; wood, $75; hardware, $30

SHOPPING LIST

144 feet 1×2 pine
48 feet 1×4 pine
20 feet 2×4
One 4×8 sheet ⅜-inch CDX plywood
Four 2-inch ball-bearing casters
6 pair 1½-inch × 1½-Inch steel hinges
#8 × 3-inch galvanized screws
#6 × 2-inch galvanized screws
#6 × 1-inch galvanized screws
¾-inch wire brads
12 square feet ½-inch mesh hardware cloth
36 square feet single-strength window glass
9 square feet ⅛-inch acrylic sheet

PROJECT SPECS

The greenhouse cabinet measures
27½ inches deep by 35½ inches wide by 76 inches high.

RAIL DETAIL

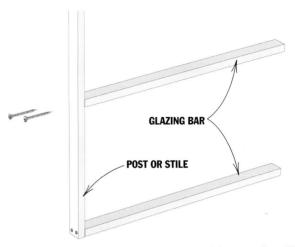

GLAZING BAR

POST OR STILE

Pairs of 2-inch screws hold the cabinet joints together. All the joints in the greenhouse sides and doors are made the same way.

CUTTING LIST

PART	QTY.	DIMENSIONS	NOTES
Base side	2	1½ × 3½ × 36	2×4
Base end	2	1½ × 3½ × 22¾	2×4
Base rail	3	1½ × 3½ × 33	2×4
Back	1	⅜ × 36 × 76	Fir plywood
Bottom	1	⅜ × 25¾ × 36	Piece from plywood offcuts
Base fascia	1	¾ × 4 × 36	
Front corner post	2	¾ × 1½ × 72	Miter one end 12½°
Rear corner post	2	¾ × 1½ × 66¾	Miter one end 12½°
Glazing bar	12	¾ × 1½ × 24	Standard 1×2
Back cap	1	¾ × 1½ × 33	Trim to fit
Side cap	1	¾ × 1½ × 25	Miter both ends 12½°
Front cap	1	¾ × 2¼ × 33	Trim to fit
Door stile	4	¾ × 1½ × 65	Standard 1×2
Door glazing bar	12	¾ × 1½ × 15⅜	Standard 1×2
Glazing strip		¼ × ¾ × 240 feet	Cut to fit
Skylight long rail	3	¾ × 1½ × 37¼	
Skylight side rail	3	¾ × 1½ × 25	
Skylight outer side rail	2	¾ × 1½ × 29	
Shelf stile	4	¾ × 1¾ × 32½	
Shelf rail	6	¾ × 1¾ × 23	
Shelf support	8	¾ × ¾ × 22	
Door stop	1	¾ × ¾ × 9	
Side pane	10	11⅞ × 23⅞	Single-strength window glass
Door pane	10	11⅞ × 15¼	Single-strength window glass
Skylight	1	⅛ × 31 × 39	Acrylic sheet
Vent pane	2	6 × 23⅞	Cut to fit

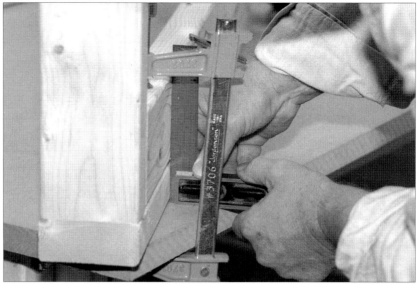

Build the base. Clamp the base side to the bench, bring the end piece square to it, and clamp it down as well. Then drill pilot holes and screw the pieces together.

Make the bottom. Spread glue on the wheels base rail, clamp it inside the base frame, then screw it in place (above). Roll glue onto the base frame. Screw the plywood to the frame (below).

BUILDING THE GREENHOUSE CABINET

1 Cut all the wood. The cabinet sides and doors are made from standard 1×2 lumber, which is ¾ inches thick and 1⅝ inches wide. The cabinet base is made from standard 2×4, while the back and bottom come out of a sheet of ⅜-inch exterior plywood. The glass retaining strips measure ¼ inch thick by ¾ inch wide. You can buy stock molding of this dimension, but it's expensive. We sawed the glass retaining strips from 1×4 lumber, with the table saw rip fence set to the finished thickness of ¼ inch. You must use a push stick for this cut. Crosscut the lumber to exact length before you saw it into strips.

2 Build the base. The base has to bear the stress of wheeling the cabinet around your deck or patio, so it should be sturdy. It's made of 2×4s, joined with two

3-inch screws in each corner. Drill pilot holes through the face of the long base side, so the screws go into the end grain of the end piece, as shown in the top left photo.

3 Make the bottom. Arrange two plywood offcuts on the 2×4 base, and trim them to a neat fit. Where they meet locates the center base rail, so make a layout line on the 2×4 base. The other two base rails support the wheels. They're turned on edge, then glued and screwed to the 2×4 base, with 3-inch screws. Roll glue onto the edge of the wheels rail. Clamp the rail in place as shown in the top right photo, then drill pilot holes into each end and drive a pair of

BUILDING THE CABINET SIDES

To build the cabinet sides, screw the first glazing bar to the back corner post. Use the 12-inch gauge to space the next glazing bar. Join all the glazing bars, then add the front post and the side cap. Build the doors in the same way.

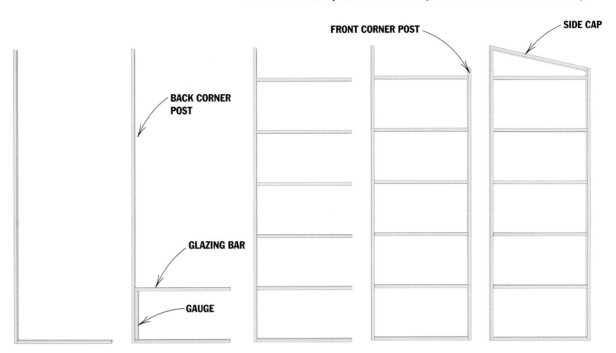

FRONT CORNER POST

SIDE CAP

BACK CORNER POST

GLAZING BAR

GAUGE

screws. Drive three more screws through the side of the base into the edge of the rail. Screw the center rail to the base sides, then attach the plywood with glue and finishing nails.

4 Make the sides. Each side consists of a front and back corner post connected by six glazing bars. The corner posts are screwed to the glazing bars with two 2-inch screws in each joint. The screws go through the posts and into the end grain of the glazing bars. Begin at the bottom corner, but make sure the top miters are correctly oriented, that is, parallel with their long points toward the back of the cabinet, as shown on the next page. Clamp the back post and the first glazing bar to the worktable. Check for square, then drill pilot holes and drive the first two screws. Since all the glass openings are 12 inches

Make the sides. Clamp the corner post to the worktable. Use a gauge to space the glazing bars. Drive two screws into each joint.

high, saw a 12-inch gauge from 1×2 wood. Use the gauge to locate each glazing bar. Attach the front post to the free ends of the glazing bars in the same way. Use the gauge to locate each joint, and check for square before you drill for the screws.

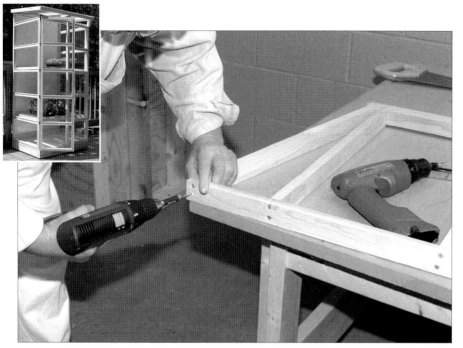

Miter the side cap. Hold the side cap in place to mark and saw the miter. Drill pilot holes and drive two screws through each intersection.

Join the back and base. Support the plywood on the worktable while you screw it to the base.

SIDE DETAIL

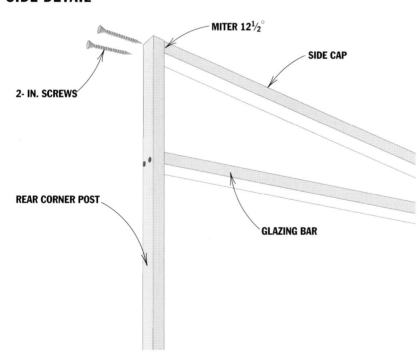

MITER 12½°

SIDE CAP

2- IN. SCREWS

REAR CORNER POST

GLAZING BAR

The side cap fits between the front and rear corner posts. Miter one end and hold the part in position to lay out the other end. Saw the second miter and screw the cap in place.

5 Miter the side cap. The side cap completes the sides. It fits between the corner posts with a matching miter at each end. The length given, 25 inches, is nominal. Miter one end 12½ degrees and hold the cap in position to lay out and cut the second miter.

6 Join the back and base. Glue and screw the plywood back to the 2×4 base. Roll glue onto the base, then position the plywood flush with the bottom edge of the base. Draw a layout line and drive 12 of the 1¼-inch screws through the plywood into the base.

7 Join the sides. Lift the back-and-base assembly onto the worktable and clamp the first side in position. Make sure the side will clamp up square—there's a little room to wiggle in every direction. When it's right, draw a layout line on the plywood, take the side down, and roll glue onto the plywood. Clamp the side to the base and back, and screw it down. Screw down through the bottom glazing bar into the base, making sure to countersink the screwheads, because if they contact the glass, it will break. Screw through the plywood back into the ends of the glazing bars with 2-inch screws, then drive a 1-inch screw at the center of each glass opening.

Join the sides. Roll glue on the plywood, then screw the cabinet together.

Trim the back cap. Rasp the corner off the plywood and back cap to match the slope of the side cap (below).

8 Trim the back cap. Trim the back cap to fit between the corner posts, then glue and screw it to the plywood back. Use a Surform, a rasp or a plane to bevel the top edge of the back cap, so it matches the slope of the sides, as shown at right.

9 Fit the front cap. Trim the front cap to fit between the front corner posts. Take the measurement at the bottom of the door opening, not at the top. Screw the front cap to the top of the door opening. It not only braces the cabinet opening, but it also acts as a stop or kicker for the doors.

10 Complete the base. The cabinet mounts on four ordinary 2-inch utility casters, which fit inside the corners of the base. Lay the cabinet on its back to screw the wheels to the base rails. Make sure the casters have room to pivot freely. Nail the base fascia on the front of the base, covering the edge of the plywood.

Complete the base. Screw the casters to the wheel rail under the base. Set them in from the sides so they can pivot freely.

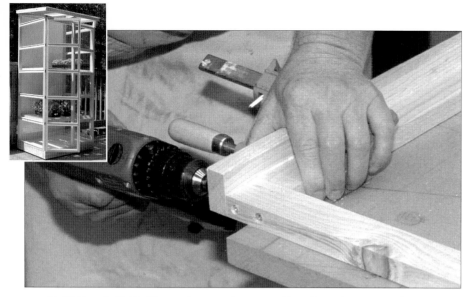

Build the skylight. Glue and screw the outer side rails to the skylight frame (above). Drill oversized clearance holes for the screws that attach the acrylic to the skylight frame. Drill the acrylic with an ordinary twist bit (below left).

Glaze the cabinet. Nail glazing strips around all of the openings, fit the glass, then nail the second set of glazing strips on the outside of the glass.

BUILDING THE SKYLIGHT

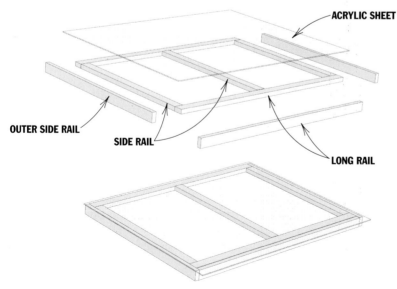

ACRYLIC SHEET

OUTER SIDE RAIL

SIDE RAIL

LONG RAIL

11 Make the doors. The two doors are made in exactly the same way as the cabinet sides, minus the mitered cap strip. Be sure you use the same 12-inch gauge to position each door glazing bar on the door stiles.

12 Build the skylight. The skylight is a square frame hinged to the cabinet. It's got overhanging front and side rails, and it's completely covered with a sheet of acrylic plastic, so it's reasonably weathertight. Lay two of the side rails and two of the long rails flat on the worktable and screw them together with two 3-inch screws through each joint. Glue and screw the outer side rails to the frame, turning them up on edge so they make a flange. Glue and screw the third side rail across the center of the skylight opening and the third long rail across the front between the outer side rails. Fit the skylight onto the cabinet and fasten it with two 1½-inch × 1½-inch galvanized hinges. Finally, screw the acrylic plastic to the top of the skylight frame. The plastic fits flush with the sides, but it overhangs 1½ inches at the front and ½ inch at the back.

13 Glaze the cabinet. The glass is trapped between pairs of glazing strips nailed to the doors and cabinet sides. Fasten the strips with ¾-inch wire brads, four in each horizontal strip and three in each vertical. Begin by nailing the glazing strips all around the inside of all the openings. These strips fit flush with the inside faces of the doors and cabinet sides. Working one opening at a time, set the glass in place, then nail the outside strips into the

GLAZING

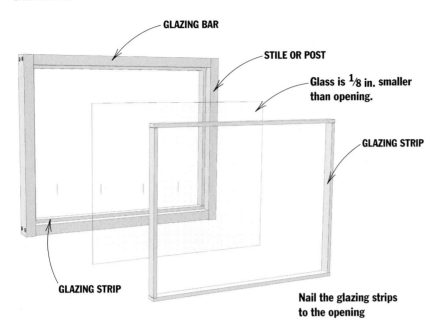

GLAZING BAR

STILE OR POST

Glass is $\frac{1}{8}$ in. smaller than opening.

GLAZING STRIP

GLAZING STRIP

Nail the glazing strips to the opening

Hang the doors. Screw the hinges onto the door, then screw them to the corner posts. The hinges will cover the screwheads in the frames.

openings, tight against the glass. The strips will protrude $\frac{1}{8}$ inch, creating a shadow reveal around each glass pane, as shown at top right.

14 Hinge the doors. Hinge each door to the front corner post with six $1\frac{1}{2} \times 1\frac{1}{2}$-inch hinges. Locate the hinges at the ends of the glazing strips, flush with the outside edge of the corner post, as shown at top right. This gives the most support to the door, and it also conceals the screws in the cabinet sides.

15 Triangular openings. There are two triangular openings at the top of the cabinet sides. What you do about them depends on your climate and growing plans. We cut triangular pieces of glass, sizing the glass to leave $\frac{1}{8}$ inch of clearance. You could fill them with wood or plastic, or you could leave them open for ventilation.

Make the shelves. Staple wire mesh onto the shelves. Rasp the sharp ends off the wire mesh.

16 Make the shelves. The shelves are simple wooden frames screwed together like the cabinet sides and doors. With the doors fully open, they slide straight into the cabinet. They're covered with $\frac{1}{2}$-inch wire mesh or hardware cloth. Cut the mesh with wire cutters, and wear leather gloves because the ends are sharp. Nail it or staple it to the wood. Rasp the

Support the shelves. Center the shelf supports on the inside of the glazing bars and screw them in place.

sharp ends off the wire, as shown in the photo above.

17 Support the shelves. The shelf supports are square sticks of wood screwed to the inside of the glazing bars. They don't go all the way back, so it's possible to brush them clean of debris. Finally, screw a 9-inch scrap to the bottom of the opening, to act as a door stop.

GARDEN GATE

This swinger makes a clean break between yard and garden

The garden gate makes a transition from the yard to the vegetable patch or flower garden. It's not a security apparatus so it doesn't have to be massive. It's a visual device, and perhaps a deer barrier. The width of the gate is up to you, and since its function is visual, the arrangement of the slats gives you an opportunity to play. You can vary the number and width of the slats, their spacing, and their height.

Glue and #6 × 1-inch galvanized construction screws hold the gate together. You don't see the screws from the front because they're all driven from the back side. This means you assemble the gate face-down on the worktable. You don't see most of the screws from the back side either, because they're hidden under the hinge rail, which goes on last.

Because this project requires sawing wood lengthwise, and also sawing bevels, it's designed for the table saw. However, the bevels and the variations in width are aesthetic, not structural. You could eliminate them and make a modified gate by cutting the wood to length with a chopsaw, a portable circular saw, or a hand saw.

GARDEN GATE

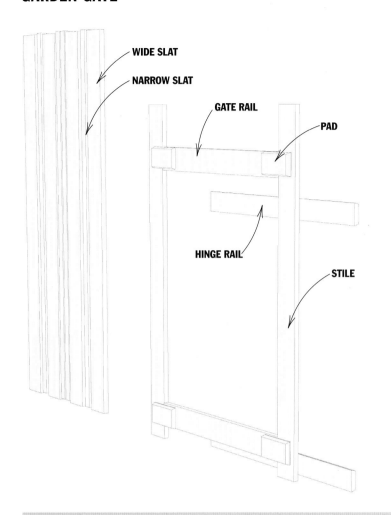

WIDE SLAT

NARROW SLAT

GATE RAIL

PAD

HINGE RAIL

STILE

JOINT DETAIL

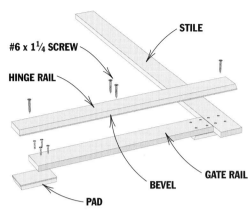

#6 x 1¼ SCREW

HINGE RAIL

STILE

BEVEL

GATE RAIL

PAD

Center the pad on the end of the gate rail.

The pads hold the construction together by bridging the butt joint between the gate rails and stiles. The slat dimensions and spacing are up to you.

BUILDING THE GARDEN GATE

1 Saw all the parts. All the material comes out of 1×4 pine lumber. The two hinge rails and the four pads, which hold the gate together, have a 15° bevel on three edges, with the fourth edge left square. To make the hinge rails, start with two 32-inch lengths of clear wood. Tilt your table saw to 15° and bevel one long edge of each piece, then set the saw's fence 3 inches from the blade and bevel the other long edge. To make the beveled pads, start with a 24-inch length of clear wood, and bevel it to match the hinge rails. Leave the table saw blade tilted

YOUR INVESTMENT
<u>Time:</u> One afternoon
<u>Money:</u> $35

SHOPPING LIST
40 feet of 1×4 pine
20 feet of 1×1 pine
Two galvanized strap hinges
#6 × 1¼-inch galvanized construction screws
#6 × 2-inch galvanized construction screws

PROJECT SPECS
The gate shown is 32 inches wide and 53 inches high.

CUTTING LIST

PART	QTY.	DIMENSIONS	NOTES
Stile	2	¾ × 3½ × 48	1×4
Gate rail	2	¾ × 3½ × 25½	Vary length to gate opening
Pad	4	¾ × 3 × 5	Bevel 15°
Wide slat	4	¾ × 3½ × 52	1×4
Narrow slat	4	1 × 1 × 52	
Hinge rail	2	¾ × 3 × 31½	Bevel 15°

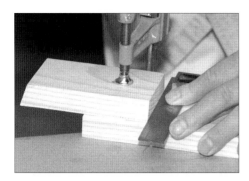

Join the stile and rails. Spread glue on the pad and the end of the gate rails, clamp them to the stile, check for square, then screw the joints together.

Attach the second stile. Clamp the parts together and drive one screw through each joint, then measure the diagonals. When they are equal, the frame is square and you can drive the rest of the screws.

Join the pads and gate rails. Spread glue on the bottom of the pad, then use a square to align it with the end of the rail (top). Clamp it in place. Turn the parts over and make the joint with four screws (bottom).

at 15° and use the saw's miter gauge to crosscut one end of the hinge rail, and also to crosscut the pads blank into four 5½ inch pieces. Finally, square up the saw blade to crosscut the other end of the hinge rails, and of the four pad blanks, to their finished lengths.

2 Join the pads and gate rails. The pads hold the gate together by bridging the butt joint between the horizontal gate rails and the stiles, or vertical posts. The first step is to glue and screw the pads to the ends of the gate rails. Find the center of each pad and square a line across. Align a pad on the end of a gate rail, as shown in the photo above, so it overlaps by half its length with the pad's square end on the gate rail and its beveled end extending into

space. Spread glue on the pad, then screw the two pieces together with four of the 1¼-inch screws. Attach the other three pads in exactly the same way.

3 Join the stile and rails. Choose which sides of the stiles you want to face front, and lay both stiles face-down on the worktable. Begin at the bottom of one stile. The bottom gate rail lands 2 inches up from the ends of the stiles. Align the parts with a square as shown at top right, and draw layout lines. Spread glue on the mating sur-

faces, clamp the assembly to the table, drill pilot holes and drive four screws through the joint from the back side. The top gate rail sits 6 inches down from the end of the stile. Align it, glue it, clamp it, and screw it.

4 Attach the second stile. The remaining stile should drop perfectly into place, making a square frame. Spread glue, clamp the parts together, then drive one screw through each of the two joints. As shown in the bottom photo, check the diagonals of the frame with

Screw the first two slats to the frame. Clamp the slats against the pads. Drive two screws through each gate rail into the slat.

Add two more wide slats. Use a 2-inch spacer block, top right, to align the slats. Draw layout lines, then glue and screw the parts together.

Attach the narrow slats. Slide the narrow slats into the spaces and line them up with the wide slats. Spread glue and screw them to the gate rails.

your tape measure. If they are equal, the frame is square, so drive three more screws through each joint. If they are not equal, push one corner square to the frame, clamp up, and drive the remaining screws.

5 Screw the first two slats to the frame. Four wide slats and four narrow ones fill in the center of the gate. The first two wide slats butt tightly against the square ends of the pads. They're set up 1 inch from the bottom of the stiles. Draw layout lines, then spread glue and screw the slats to the gate rails.

6 Add two more wide slats. To align the remaining two wide slats, use a pair of 2-inch spacer blocks made from scrap wood, as shown in the top middle photo. This will leave a wide center gap between the slats, which you'll fill in the next step. Glue and screw the slats to the gate rails, with two screws through each joint.

7 Attach the narrow slats. Slide the narrow slats into

Add the hinge rails. The square end of the hinge rails goes to the hinge side. Glue and screw the hinge rails to the back of the gate rails.

place and space them however you like. We spaced them $\frac{5}{8}$ inch from the wide slats. Draw layout lines, spread glue within the layout lines, and drive a total of four screws through the gate rails into each narrow slat.

8 Add the hinge rails. You have to decide now whether the gate will be hinged right-handed or left-handed, because the square ends of the hinge rails are what supports the

hinges. The square ends fit flush with the edge of the stile. Spread glue all across the gate rails, and screw each hinge rail down with four 2-inch screws.

9 Finish the gate. Once you've installed the gate in its fence, you'll probably want to add a latch and sand off the sharp edges where people will be handling the wood. Then stain the gate to match the fence, or leave it alone to darken in the weather.

GARDEN FENCE

Tailor the decorative slats to suit your own taste

Here is an attractive garden fence you can make yourself. It features a modular system of posts and fence panels. You can tailor the decorative details to suit your own taste, without changing the structure of the fence.

A garden fence is a big project, but you get a lot of help from the metal post stakes that have recently shown up at the home centers. These welded steel devices allow you to set a sturdy post wherever you need one, without the hard work of digging post holes and planting posts in them. They also hold the post off the damp ground and allow it to drain, so it won't rot and you don't need to work with pressure-treated wood.

As an alternative to making the whole fence, you can also get a lot of help from manufactured fence panels. While there is a great variety of fence panels at the home center, there's a shortage of interesting designs. So one way to approach a fence project is to make your own posts, then fill in with the home center's panels. The project on

FENCE PANEL

Glue up the stile pieces, forming a wide rabbet. Fasten the rails to the rabbet, then screw the decorative slats to the rails. The slat widths and spacing are up to you.

POST

Construct the post around the 4x4 stub, then add the cap, trim and retainers.

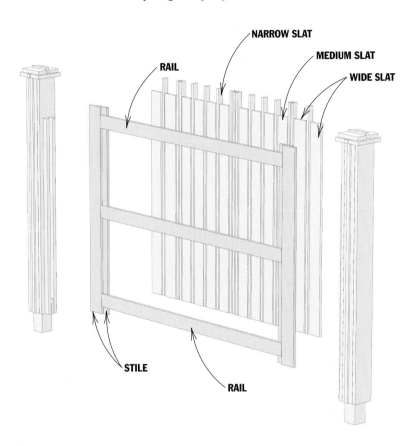

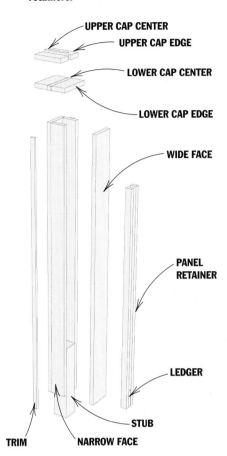

YOUR INVESTMENT

<u>Time:</u> All weekend
<u>Money:</u> Post, $22; metal stake, $15; fence panel, $70

PROJECT SPECS

The top of the installed fence post is 6 feet high. Each fence panel is 6 feet wide and 5 feet high.

SHOPPING LIST

POST
2 feet 4×4 fir
16 feet 1×2 pine
16 feet 1×4 pine
16 feet 1×6 pine
#8 × 3-inch galvanized spiral nails
2½-inch galvanized siding nails

FENCE PANEL
70 feet 1×2 pine
60 feet 1×4 pine
50 feet 1×5 pine
#6 × 1¼-inch galvanized screws

CUTTING LIST

PART	QTY.	DIMENSION	NOTES
FENCE PANEL			
Rail	3	$\frac{3}{4} \times 3\frac{1}{2} \times 72$	1×4
Stile	4	$\frac{3}{4} \times 4\frac{1}{2} \times 56$	1×5
Narrow slat	12	$\frac{3}{4} \times 1\frac{1}{2} \times 60$	1×2
Medium slat	6	$\frac{3}{4} \times 3\frac{1}{2}2 \times 56$	1×4
Wide slat	6	$\frac{3}{4} \times 4\frac{1}{2} \times 56$	1×5
POST			
Stub	1	$3\frac{5}{8} \times 3\frac{5}{8} \times 18$	4×4
Narrow face	2	$1 \times 3\frac{5}{8} \times 65$	1×4
Wide face	2	$1 \times 5\frac{5}{8} \times 65$	1×6
Lower cap center	1	$1 \times 1 \times 8\frac{1}{2}$	
Lower cap edge	2	$1 \times 3\frac{1}{2} \times 8$	1×4
Upper cap center	1	$1 \times 1\frac{1}{2} \times 6$	1×2
Upper cap edge	2	$1 \times 3 \times 7$	1×4
Trim	2	$\frac{1}{2} \times 1 \times 65$	
Panel retainer	2	$1 \times 1\frac{1}{2} \times 54$	1×2
Ledger	1	$1 \times 1\frac{1}{2} \times 4$	1×2

these pages includes both a post and a fence panel, so you can go either way. There's a matching gate on page 64.

A two-part post is the key to using the metal post stake. A short stub of 4×4 fits the cup in the metal stake. The decorative outer post is a hollow construction built right around the stub. The post shown is made of rough-sawn pine. You can substitute smooth pine boards from the home center.

The fence panels consist of a rail-and-stile framework, glued and screwed together, with the decorative slats attached to the horizontal rails. The fence panel is made of regular pine lumber.

Two panel retainer strips and a ledger connect the vertical stiles of the fence panels to the posts. This method gives the fence panel a couple of inches in which to float, in case your posts aren't quite vertical or perfectly spaced.

The modular fence panels can be made to a height and width that suits your situation, and the slats can be spaced to meet your privacy needs. Though 8-foot wide panels are standard in the fencing business, the 6-footers detailed in this project are easier to manage. You can tailor the height as well, but be sure to check the local building code because it may restrict how high you can go. The panels shown here are 5 feet high, and are designed to sit 9 inches off the ground. Although the post and panel system has a number of small adjustments built into it, it's designed for level ground, not for sloped or hilly terrain.

BUILDING THE FENCE

1 Cut the wood. There is a lot of wood in one fence panel. If you are attempting to fence a considerable distance, it will be worthwhile to figure the total amount of wood you will need and see whether you can't get a quantity deal, either from your regular lumber retailer or from a small local sawmill. To minimize waste, buy 10-foot lengths.

2 Assemble the stiles. The stiles, which anchor the fence panels at the posts, each consist of two overlapped pieces of wood. The overlap is 2½ inches, as shown in the photo below, which creates a long and substantial rabbet. Draw a layout line, spread glue on one stile piece, set the other one place, and screw the two together with six of the 1¼-inch galvanized-screws.

Assemble the stiles. The two stile pieces overlap 2½ inches. Roll glue on both pieces (above). Screw them together with 1¼-inch screws (below).

3 Join the rails and stiles. The three rails connect the stiles. They sit on the rabbet you just glued into the stile. The top and bottom rail are inset 2 inches from the ends of the stile, and the third one is centered. Locate and square one end of each rail in turn, glue it and fasten it with three of the 1¼-inch screws. Then fasten the free ends of the rails to the rabbet in the second stile. This completes the structural framework of the fence panel.

4 Attach the slats. Screw the decorative slats to the rails. Leave the framework on the worktable the way it was when you finished fastening the rails to the stiles, with the screwheads uppermost. This is the back side of the fence panel. Now you can arrange the decorative slats the way you want them to be. The arrangement of narrow, medium and wide slats, shown in the photo below, is only one of dozens of workable designs. When you settle on an arrangement you like, slip the decorative slats underneath the rails, locate and square each one up, and screw it tight to the three rails. Put two of the 1¼-inch screws into each rail. Start with the center slat and work toward both ends of the panel.

Join the rails and stiles. Fit the three rails into the glued-up rabbet (left). Glue and screw the rails to the stiles. Be sure each rail is square to the stile (above). Glue and screw the free ends of the rails to the second stile (below).

Attach the slats. Screw through the rails into the decorative slats. Start at the center of the fence and work toward the ends (above). Gauge the space between the slats with wooden spacers (below).

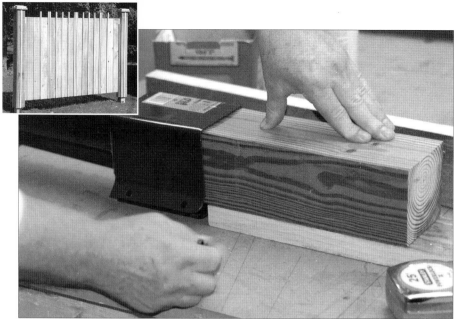

Fasten the narrow faces to the stub. Begin by squaring a line around the stub to mark the top of the stake's metal cup.

Fasten the narrow faces to the stub. Glue and nail the first narrow face to the stub (above). Use a second piece of 4×4 to support the second narrow face, while you align it with the speed square (below left).

Fasten the wide faces to the narrow ones. Glue and nail the wide faces to the edges of the narrow ones. Nail into the stub as well.

BUILDING THE POSTS

1 Cut the wood. The posts shown in the photos are made of rough-sawn pine lumber, which is about an inch thick. To minimize waste, buy the wood in 6-foot and 12-foot lengths. You can substitute smooth-planed pine from the home center. You'll have to decide whether to saw the wide faces to width, or to allow any extra width to form a reveal.

2 Fasten the narrow faces to the stub. The narrow post faces match the width of the 4×4 stub. Square a layout line around the stub to represent the top of the cup atop the metal stake. Roll a generous coating of glue on the stub, and spike the first of the two narrow post faces to it with six 3-inch spiral nails. Glue and nail the other post face on the opposite side of the stub. Align the edges of the face with the

stub, drive the first nail and pause to check the alignment at the top end, as shown in the photo above.

3 Fasten the wide faces to the narrow ones. The wide post faces bridge the narrow ones. Roll a generous coating of glue on the edges of the narrow faces and on the stub. Nail the first wide face to one side, then nail the second one to the other side.

Space the 3-inch nails a hand-span apart, and drive six more nails through each wide face into the post stub itself.

4 Cap the post. The decorative cap consists of two layers of wood running at right angles to one another. Each layer is made up of three pieces, a center and two edges. Assemble the cap with glue and siding nails right on the post. Start with the bottom center piece. Center it across the post, glue it, and nail it to the ends of the post faces as shown in the photo at right. Then butt-glue and nail the two bottom edge pieces to the center piece. Hold the three top cap pieces in position to see how they fit, and draw a layout line. Glue and nail them to the post, as shown in the photo at center.

5 Add the panel retainers and ledger. The vertical panel retainers form a groove down the side of the post, into which you can fit the fence panel. The ledger supports the weight of the panel. Glue and nail the panel retainers to the side of the post, but be sure to use a sample of your actual panel material to gauge the width of the groove. Then glue and nail the ledger into the bottom of the slot between the retainers. Nail through the ledger into the post face, and also nail through the retainers into the ledger.

6 Trim the post. The trim pieces run down two faces of the post, as visual extensions of the bottom center cap. Spread glue on each trim piece, center it on the post face, and nail it to the post with the siding nails.

Cap the post. Glue and nail the lower center cap piece to the top of the post (above). Butt the lower cap edges up to the center piece (right). Glue and nail the upper cap to the lower cap (below).

Add the panel retainers and ledger. Glue and nail the panel retainers to one face of the post (above). Fit the ledger into the bottom of the slot between the retainers (right).

INSTALLING YOUR FENCE

There is a general strategy for installing a fence. The method is to establish the line of the fence, then to make the line level, and finally to locate the posts along the level line.

Begin at the end nearest the house and drive a stake in the ground. Tie a string over the top of the first stake and stretch it along the proposed line of the fence. Drive a second stake on the line of the fence, the length of your level away from the original stake. Use the longest level you have. If what you have is short, tape it to the middle of a straight 8-foot 2×4. Set the long level across the top of the two stakes and lift one end up and down to see how far off it is. Drive the second stake until its top is level with the top of the original stake.

Drive a third stake at the other end of the proposed fence. Now you can sight the string from the first stake, across the top of the second stake, to the third stake. Adjust the string and the third stake to create a straight and level line, and tie the string taut.

Finally, locate the posts by measuring along the string. You can mark the posts with wooden stakes, but it's easiest to go directly to the metal stakes themselves. Start with the gate post closest to the middle of the fence. Decide where you want it to be and start the metal stake into the

Drive a stake at one end of the proposed fence.

Tie a string over the top of the first stake (above). Tape it so it can't slip.

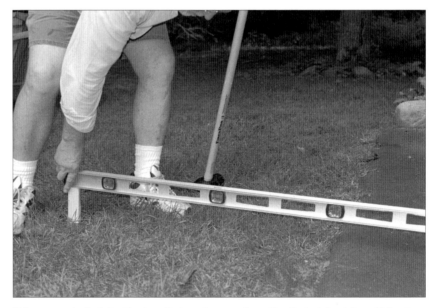

Drive a second stake the level's length away from the first. Adjust it until the two stakes are level.

ground, using a 4×4 stub as an anvil. Drive it down about a foot, then use your level to make it as vertical and plumb as you can as shown in the photos on the facing page. Continue to drive the stake until the base of its cup sits at ground level.

With the first stake in place, note where the level string falls relative to the top of the cup. Measure the width of your fence panel or gate and measure along the string to locate the next metal stake. Be sure to allow for the difference between the width

Drive the third stake at the other end of the fence. Adjust the string so it grazes the top of the second or center stake. Tie the string off level.

Measure the width of the gate and drive the second metal stake.

Locate the first fence post and drive the metal stake into the ground.

Use the level to make sure the metal stake is vertical.

Set the fence post in the metal stake. Make sure it is plumb.

of the wooden post and the width of the metal stake. Drive the stake into the ground, checking carefully for alignment as you go. Drive it down until the string crosses the metal cup in the same place as on the first stake.

Now you can proceed along the line of the fence, driving each stake down level with the string.

If the ground rises a bit, you might have to dig a hole, and if the ground falls, you'll have to mound it up around the stake.

When you install the fence posts in the metal stakes, make sure they are vertical. If one is really off, you might have to uproot it and replant it, as shown in the photo at right.

To adjust a metal stake, you may have to uproot it and reset it. Pry it out of the ground with a 2×4 lever.

GARDEN GATEWAY

Arts-and-Crafts design opens a path between outdoor rooms

A graceful gateway defines the spaces in your outdoor living area. It helps you organize your yard and garden into "rooms." When people pass through a gateway, they expect a change of place: from lawn to flower garden, from playground to patio, from one side of the lawn to the other.

This gateway consists of two archways connected by decorative side panels. The strong vertical lines of the grilles in the side panels suggest Arts-and-Crafts furniture. There are seven grille pieces, and seven rafters. You can change the dimensions of the gateway to suit your own tastes, and you might want to change the number of grille and rafter pieces. However, if you do,

keep the number odd, so one piece always falls on center. It looks better that way.

You can set a gateway in a fence or hedge, and you can hang a gate in it. But you can also set a gateway out in your yard without any fence or gate, on a pathway or on the lawn. Like the Arc de Triomphe in Paris, it creates spaces just by being there.

GARDEN GATEWAY

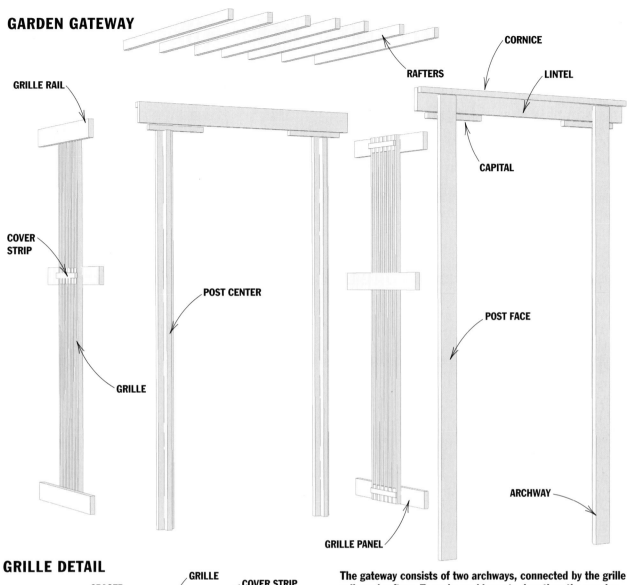

The gateway consists of two archways, connected by the grille rails and rafters. To make a wider gate, lengthen the cornice and lintel, and add pairs of rafters. To make a longer passage through the gate, lengthen the rafters and grille rails, and add pairs of grilles. If you decide to change the height of the posts, adjust the grilles as well.

GRILLE DETAIL

YOUR INVESTMENT

<u>Time:</u> One day
<u>Money:</u> $35

SHOPPING LIST

125 feet 1×4 rough-sawn pine
#6 × 1⅝-inch galvanized screws
#6 × 2-inch galvanized screws
1½-inch galvanized finishing nails
1½-inch galvanized spiral nails
2-inch galvanized spiral nails
2½-inch galvanized spiral nails

PROJECT SPECS

The gateway stands 84 inches high,
42 inches wide, and 28 inches deep.

CUTTING LIST

PART	QTY.	DIMENSIONS	NOTES
Post face	4	$1 \times 3\frac{3}{8} \times 81$	
Post center	4	$1 \times 1\frac{1}{2} \times 77$	
Lintel	2	$1 \times 4 \times 48$	
Capital	4	$1 \times 1 \times 12$	
Cornice	2	$1 \times 1 \times 48$	
Grille	14	$\frac{1}{2} \times 1 \times 72$	
Grille spacer	36	$1 \times 1 \times 3$	
Grille rail	6	$1 \times 3\frac{3}{8} \times 26$	
Rafter	7	$1 \times 1\frac{1}{8} \times 46$	
Cover strip	6	$\frac{1}{2} \times 1 \times 12$	Trim to fit

Make the posts. Glue and clamp the post center to the post face. The end offset is the width of the lintel (above). Turn the assembly over and nail through from the back. Angle the nails for the best grip (right).

BUILDING THE GATEWAY

1 Saw the parts. Rough-sawn pine, which is available in most parts of the country, not only looks good against green plants, but it's also a full inch in thickness. Thicker looks better, but nowhere is the thickness of the wood a critical dimension. You can substitute lumberyard 1× pine, which is about ¾ inch thick, or the more robust 5/4 pine, which is actually about 1⅛ inches thick. Saw all the parts before you begin construction. The ½-inch grille pieces and the various 1-inch and 2-inch parts can be sawn lengthwise from 1×4 material. If you don't have a table saw for cutting the wood lengthwise, substitute 1×1 and 1×2 lumber for the grilles, cornices, and capitals.

2 Make the posts. The four posts, T-shaped in cross-section, are two-piece assemblies. The

Join the lintel and capitals. Set the capital 2 inches in from the end of the lintel (above).Nail the capitals to the lintels (right).

post center is shorter than the post face by the width of the lintel, or 4 inches. Spread glue on the edge of the post center and clamp the two parts together. Make them fit flush at the bottom, then measure to make sure the offset at the top is the actual width of your lintel. Nail through the post face into the post center with 2½-inch spiral nails. It's easiest to make all four posts at the same time.

3 Join the lintel and capitals. The little capitals make the visual transition between the horizontal lintels and the vertical posts. Glue and nail two capitals to the edge of each lintel. Set them 2 inches in from the ends of the lintel.

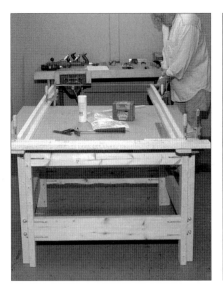

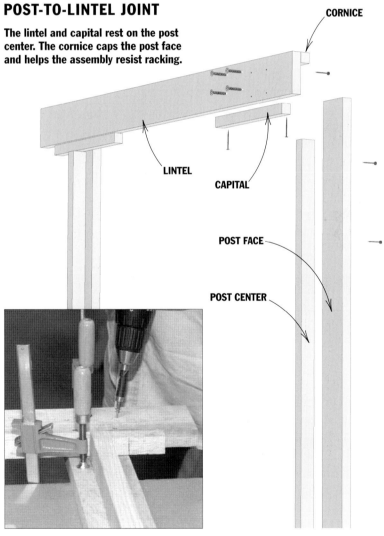

Connect the posts. Clamp the lintel to the posts and measure for equal width at top and bottom (left). Screw a scrap strip across the bottom, then measure the diagonals (right). To square the gateway, shift the parts until the diagonals are equal.

4 **Connect the posts.** Each lintel spans two posts, with its capitals resting on the post center pieces. Lay the two posts on the worktable and clamp them down. Set the lintel-and-capital assembly in place across the posts. Locate the outside edge of the posts 2 inches in from the ends of the capitals. Clamp the assembly together. Check for parallel by measuring the distance between the posts at top and bottom. Cut a scrap stick to the distance between the center pieces and screw it across the bottom of the gateway. Check for square by measuring the diagonals. Now spread glue and screw through the face of the lintel into the posts, with four of the 1⅝-inch screws in each joint.

5 **Add the cornice.** The cornice is a horizontal strip of wood glued and nailed to the lintel and resting atop the posts. Spread glue on the cornice piece, clamp it in place, and nail into it through the face of the lintel, with the 1⅝ inch nails. Build the second archway in the same way.

POST-TO-LINTEL JOINT

The lintel and capital rest on the post center. The cornice caps the post face and helps the assembly resist racking.

CORNICE

LINTEL

CAPITAL

POST FACE

POST CENTER

Connect the posts. Screw through the lintel into the post face.

Space the grilles. Roll glue and nail the first set of spacer blocks to the first grille (left). Continue to add grilles and spacers to complete the grille panel (right).

Add the grille rails. Center the grilles on the top grille rail and check for square (above). Screw the spacer blocks to the grille rails (right).

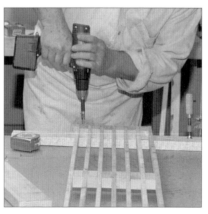

6 Space the grilles. The grille panels fill in the sides of the gateway. Each panel consists of seven grilles separated by three sets of spacer blocks. Glue and nail the first set of three spacers to one grille, using the 1¼-inch finishing nails. The two end spacers fit flush with the ends of the grille. A 24-inch gap separates the top spacer from the center spacer. Add a second grille, then glue and nail the second set of spacers to it, using 2½-inch siding nails, which are extra thin so they don't split the wood. Continue to glue and nail spacers and grilles until you complete both panels.

7 Add the grille rails. The horizontal grille rails will connect the posts, but first, glue and screw them to the grilles themselves. There's a rail at each set of spacer blocks. The top and bottom rails go on one side of the grilles, and the middle rail goes on the other. Center the grilles on the top rail, draw layout lines, and spread glue. Slip the rail into position and drive the first 1⅝-inch screw through a grille spacer into the rail. Check for square, then drive the remaining screws. Attach the bottom rail in the same way, then turn the grille panel over to attach the center rail on the other side.

8 Assemble the gateway. Stand the front and back archways up on edge, with one of them against the wall of the workshop. The grille rails span the post center pieces top, bottom and center. To keep the assembly from flopping around, clamp the grille rails to the posts, then screw them in place, with two 1⅝-inch

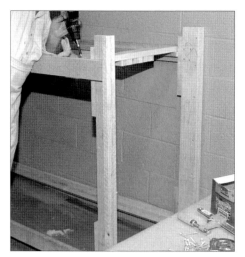

Assemble the gateway. Stand the two archways on edge, with one of them against a wall. Fit the grille panel to the posts and screw the rails in place.

Complete the rafters. Attach the outside rafters and the center rafter. Space the remaining rafters in between.

screws at each end. Rotate the assembly to attach the second grille panel.

9 Start the rafters. If you're working indoors, carry the gateway outside before you add the rafters. Afterward, it probably wouldn't fit through the doorway. The seven rafter pieces stand up on edge across the top of the cornices and lintels. The two outside rafters don't fit flush with the end of the cornice and lintel; they're set in an inch. Clamp the first rafter so you can drive 2½-inch screws up into it through the cornice. Rotate the gate to attach the companion rafter on the other side.

10 Complete the rafters. The remaining five rafters march across the top of the gateway. Locate the center rafter by measuring the distance between the two outside rafters. Screw it in place, then divide the remaining spaces into widths of pleasing proportion and screw the rest of the rafters to the cornices. The gateway shown on page 76 has

Cover the screws. Glue and nail the cover strips across the grille spacer blocks.

smaller spaces in the center, which emphasizes the opening.

11 Cover the screws. There's an unsightly row of screwheads where you attached the grilles to the grille rails. Trim the cover strips to length, then glue and nail them over the screwheads with several finishing nails.

12 Install the gateway. Set the posts on bricks or flat stones. Level the posts by leveling the supporting bricks. Then drive an 18-inch wooden stake into the ground alongside each post, and tie or screw the bottom of the post to it. Remove the scrap spreaders at the bottom of the gateway, and amble on through.

BRIDGE

Joist hangers help make a span that's strong and safe

The usual reason for building a bridge is to get across a gully or stream. However, like the gateway on page 76, a bridge doesn't have to go anywhere. It can stretch from point to point across perfectly level ground. It's reasonable to make a bridge just for fun, especially a bridge like the one shown here. This bridge is extremely strong, it's good looking, yet it's not difficult to build.

A bridge is an exercise in wood engineering, because the last thing you want is uncertainty about its strength. Every piece of wood in this bridge contributes its share of support. Even the spacers between the balusters and the main beams are structural. They not only support the balusters while allowing the deck to extend beyond the width of the bridge frame, they also help keep the main beams from twisting.

The spine of the bridge is a ladder made from standard 2×6 construction lumber, held together with nails and joist hangers. The bridge shown is just over 8 feet long, so the two main beams and the four cross beams can come out of a pair of 12-foot planks. These dimensions put the cross beams on 24-inch centers. If you decide to make a longer bridge, make the beams deeper by switching from 2×6 to 2×8 lumber. You'll also need more cross beams, but keep the spacing between 16 inches minimum and 24 inches maximum.

The deck, handrails, and balusters, or handrail supports, are made from 4/4 rough-sawn pine, which is readily obtainable from small sawmills in most parts of the country, and which measures about an inch thick. You could substitute any 4/4 rough-sawn lumber that's available in your locale; for a really tough bridge, use white oak. If you can't find rough-sawn material, you can use regular 5/4 pine lumber from the home center. It's generally about $1\frac{1}{8}$ inches thick. Making this change will require that you make the bridge decking about $\frac{1}{4}$-inch longer. You might also want to increase the width of the handrail cap by $\frac{1}{4}$ inch. The dimension given is wide enough to cover the pieces underneath, plus a shadow reveal. While you don't need the shadow reveal for any structural reason, it does help the bridge look good.

Whether you use rough-sawn lumber or 5/4 pine, you will have to saw some pieces lengthwise in

BRIDGE

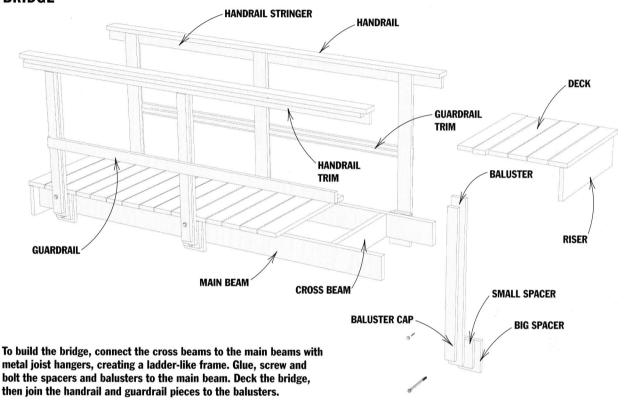

To build the bridge, connect the cross beams to the main beams with metal joist hangers, creating a ladder-like frame. Glue, screw and bolt the spacers and balusters to the main beam. Deck the bridge, then join the handrail and guardrail pieces to the balusters.

YOUR INVESTMENT

Time: All weekend
Money: $75

SHOPPING LIST

Two 12-foot 2×6 planks
150 linear feet (75 board feet) 1×6
  rough-sawn pine
Six joist hangers
$1\frac{1}{2}$-inch galvanized joist-hanger nails
Six $\frac{5}{16}$ × $3\frac{1}{2}$-inch lag bolts
  with washers
Six $\frac{5}{16}$ × $5\frac{1}{2}$-inch hex-head
  machine bolts with nuts and washers
#6 × 2-inch galvanized screws
3-inch galvanized spiral nails
2-inch galvanized siding nails

PROJECT SPECS

The bridge spans a gorge up to 6 feet wide.

CUTTING LIST

PART	QTY.	DIMENSIONS	NOTES
Main beam	2	$1\frac{1}{2}$ × $5\frac{1}{2}$ × 98	2×6
Cross beam	4	$1\frac{1}{2}$ × $5\frac{1}{2}$ × 23	2×6
Big spacer	6	1 × $5\frac{1}{2}$ × $7\frac{1}{2}$	
Small spacer	6	1 × $4\frac{1}{2}$ × $6\frac{1}{2}$	
Baluster	6	1 × $3\frac{1}{2}$ × 38	
Baluster cap	6	1 × $2\frac{1}{2}$ × $34\frac{1}{2}$	
Riser	2	1 × $5\frac{1}{2}$ × 30	
Deck	18	1 × $5\frac{1}{2}$ × $30\frac{1}{2}$	Random widths
Handrail stringer	2	1 × $2\frac{1}{2}$ × 96	
Handrail	2	1 × $3\frac{1}{2}$ × 96	
Handrail trim	2	1 × $\frac{7}{8}$ × 93	
Guardrail	2	1 × $2\frac{1}{2}$ × 81	
Guardrail trim	4	1 × 1 × 38	Trim length to fit

BUILDING THE BRIDGE

1 Make the beams. The main beams and cross beams can be sawn out of two 12-foot 2×6 planks, or else from three 8-foot 2×6 planks. When you buy the wood, look for clean material with square edges. Small, tight knots are no problem, but be sure to avoid large knots, bark-covered edges, and splits. You might have to pay extra for clean, sound wood.

2 Mount the joist hangers. Metal joist hangers connect the cross beams to the main beams. Begin by nailing joist hangers on both ends of all the cross beams. There are many varieties of joist hanger at the home center, and the little details don't much matter, so long as the type you get are designed for connecting 2×6 planks at right angles. Joist hangers are strong and forgiving, but the hanger part does have to fit tightly against the piece it's supporting. To get it right, clamp the hanger to the cross beam while you nail, as shown in the photo above. Be sure you get the hangers the same way up at either end of the cross beam.

3 Lay out the main beams. There's a cross beam 12 inches from either end of the main beams, and the cross beams are spaced 24 inches apart. Make layout marks as shown in the photo at left, and pencil an X on the main beams where you want the cross beams to fit. Lay out both main beams at the same time, because having them match is more important than precise spacing.

Mount the joist hangers. Clamp the joist hangers to the cross beams so they won't move while you nail them. Make sure the hangers are the same way up at either end of each cross beam.

Lay out the main beams. Lay out the location of the cross beams on both main beams at the same time. Making the beams match is more critical than precise spacing.

order to complete the bridge. The table saw is the tool of choice for sawing lengthwise, but as an alternative you can clamp a straight piece of wood to the workpiece to guide the cut with a portable circular saw, as shown on page 106.

If you build the bridge in the workshop, be sure you can get it out the door. It's no problem

when your workshop is in the garage, but if your shop has a regular doorway, you probably won't be able to mount the balusters before you carry the construction outside.

To install the bridge across a stream or ravine, make sure you have an adequate footing on both sides. If there's any kind of a footing in place already, use it. Otherwise, the simplest footing would be a landscaping tie set into the ground at either end of the bridge. Dig shallow trenches for the ties and bed them in gravel so their top surfaces come just above the ground. Sight across the gully from one tie to the other, and rearrange the gravel to level them as best you can. Hump the bridge into position on the ties, then spike it to them with several 3-inch nails driven on an angle.

Join the cross beams to one main beam. Place the main beam on the worktable and stand the cross beams in position. Drive one nail through the joist hanger and check for square before driving the remaining nails (left). A good fit: The joist hanger pulls the cross beam tight (above).

4 Join the cross beams to one main beam. Lay a main beam on the worktable and stand the first cross beam in position. The joist hangers have little metal positioning tabs you can hammer into the wood. Drive one nail through the joist hanger into the main beam, then check that the construction is square, and if it is not, tap it into place. Drive the rest of the nails. Join the other three cross beams to the main beam in the same way.

5 Complete the bridge frame. Lay the second main beam flat on the worktable, and stand the assembled main beam and cross beams on it. Pay attention to your layout marks, and also to keeping the top surface of the beams flush. The construction will be precarious until you nail one of the center joist hangers to the second main beam. Once one cross beam is attached at both ends, it's easy to square up

Complete the bridge frame. Lay the second main beam flat on the worktable and stand the assembled section on top of it. Nail one of the center joist hangers first, to stabilize the construction.

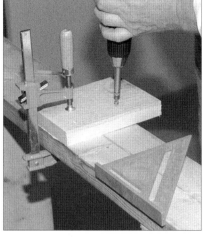

Make the first baluster support. Stand the bridge frame on edge and locate three big spacers on the main beam. Align the end spacers with the edge of the cross beams and put the third spacer in the center of the bridge frame (top left). Glue, clamp and screw the big spacers to the main beam (top right). Center the small spacer on the big spacer, flush at the top edge, and trace a layout line (below).

BALUSTER SQUARE

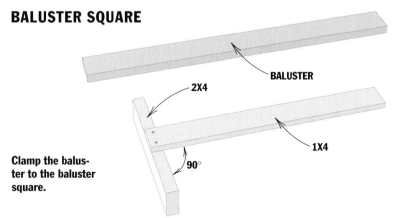

BALUSTER

2X4

1X4

90°

Clamp the baluster to the baluster square.

and nail the remaining joist hangers. This completes the frame of the bridge.

6 Make the first baluster support. The balusters are the vertical assemblies that hold up the handrails. The baluster supports connect the balusters to the main beams. Each baluster support consists of two wooden spacers glued and screwed together. Begin by standing the bridge frame on edge on the floor, so you can locate three of the big spacers on the main beam. The big spacers at the ends of the bridge line up with the edge of the cross beams. The third big spacer sits at the center of the bridge frame. Spread glue on the first big spacer, clamp it in place, and screw it to the main beam with four 2½-inch screws. Be sure the top edge of the the spacer is flush with the top edge of the main beam. Center the small spacer on the big spacer, also flush with the top edge of the main beam. Draw a layout line around the small spacer, spread glue within the layout line, clamp it, and screw it down. Use one of the balusters to lay out the four screws on the small spacer. If you keep the screws within the width of the baluster, they will be concealed.

7 Complete the baluster supports. Create the remaining five baluster supports in exactly the same way as you made the first one. It's a small point, but it's worth the trouble to examine each spacer before you spread glue on it. If it's cupped, spread the glue on the hollow side. This way, the edges are more likely to

Mount the balusters. Clamp the baluster square to the baluster (left). Plant the 2×4 arm of the baluster square onto the main beam, and the attached baluster will be correctly positioned (right).

remain tight and rainproof. In a rough softwood construction, when you clamp the parts together, you can get away without drilling clearance holes. However, if you decide not to bother with clamps, then you must drill clearance holes through the spacers. Otherwise, the screws can't pull them tight.

8 Mount the balusters. The balusters should rise vertically from the bridge deck, which means they should be at right angles to the main beams. However, since they're spaced outward by the baluster supports and offset as shown in the photo at right, there's no convenient place to fit a square. So, unless you want to measure laboriously for each of the six balusters, make a baluster square by nailing a $31\frac{1}{2}$-inch length of 1×4 to the edge of a 2×4. When you clamp the 1×4 arm to the baluster, and plant the 2×4 on the main beam, the baluster ends up in the correct place, as shown in the photo at top right. Spread glue on the baluster, clamp it to the spacer, and screw it in place with four

Bolt the balusters. Drill a $\frac{3}{8}$-inch bolt hole $\frac{5}{8}$ inch from the bottom of the baluster. Angle the hole a few degrees to make sure you catch the main beam.

$2\frac{1}{2}$-inch screws. Mount the other five balusters in the same way.

9 Bolt the balusters. To make sure the balusters stay put, bolt them to the main beams. The $5\frac{1}{2}$-inch bolt goes through the baluster, both spacers, and the main beam itself. Locate the bolt $\frac{5}{8}$ inch from the bottom of the baluster. Drill a $\frac{3}{8}$-inch hole, but angle it a few degrees in order to make sure the bolt catches the

Add the baluster caps. A lag screw driven through the baluster cap makes the construction strong and rigid. Tighten the lag screw with a wrench.

main beam, as shown in the photo above left. Tighten the bolt with a wrench, and bolt the rest of the balusters to the main beams in the same way.

10 Add the baluster caps. The baluster caps stiffen the baluster assemblies. They're glued and screwed to the outside of the balusters, then insured with a $3\frac{1}{2}$-inch lag screw. Make sure the baluster caps end $2\frac{1}{2}$ inches

Make the risers. Center and nail the vertical risers at both ends of the bridge. The top edge of the riser fits flush with the top of the beams.

Deck the bridge. Measure the actual distance between the balusters for the length of the deck boards and use whatever widths of wood you have on hand. Space the deck boards with a pair of ¼-inch slats, which are visible angling up behind the board being nailed.

from the top of the balusters themselves. This space is for the handrail stringer, which comes in Step 13. Drill a ¼-inch hole for the lag screw, located as far up the baluster cap as possible while still penetrating the baluster spacers. Drive the lag screw with a socket wrench, as shown on the previous page.

11 Make the risers. There's a vertical riser at each end of the bridge, nailed to the ends of the main beams. Center the risers from side to side, their top edges flush with the top of the beams. Nail them in place with 3-inch spiral nails.

12 Deck the bridge. The cutting list gives a nominal width for the bridge deck, but the boards can come from whatever widths of lumber you have. For the length of the deck boards, measure the actual distance between the balusters. Start decking from one end of the bridge. The first deck board overhangs the riser by about ½ inch. Use a pair of ¼-inch slats

Mount the handrail stringers. Center the handrail stringers from end to end, then glue and screw them to the balusters.

of wood to space the deck boards, as shown in the photo at top right. Attach the deck to the main beams with two 3-inch spiral nails in each end of each board. When you come to the end of the bridge, nail the last deck board to the riser before you install the next-to-last

board, which you will have to saw to fit the remaining space.

13 Mount the handrail stringer. In Step 10, you constructed a ledge at the top of the balusters, for the handrail stringer. Center each handrail stringer from end to end; they should sit on the

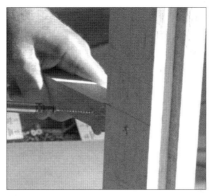

Make the guardrails. Mark a line 18 inches up from the bottom of the baluster caps for the guardrail trim. Screw the trim to the baluster (left). Roll glue onto the outside face of the guardrail trim, then clamp the guardrail to it. Screw the guardrail into the baluster caps and nail it to the guardrail trim (below).

Make the handrail. Nail the handrail into the ends of the balusters as well as into the stringers.

ends of the baluster caps and come flush with the tops of the balusters themselves. Mark where the handrail stringers fit, spread glue, clamp them in place and screw them to the balusters. Drive three 2-inch screws into each joint.

14 Make the handrails. The handrails are centered on the handrail stringers, then glued and nailed. Use the 3-inch spiral nails. Nail into the ends of the balusters as well as into the stringers. Space the nails about 9 inches apart.

15 Make the guardrails. The guardrails help keep small children from falling off the bridge. The guardrail trim stiffens the guardrails. Begin by marking a line 18 inches up from the bottom of the baluster caps. Cut the four pieces of guardrail trim to fit between the baluster caps. Drive a single $1\frac{5}{8}$-inch screw through each end of the trim, into the baluster itself. Roll glue onto the outside face of the guardrail trim and clamp the guardrail to it. Center the guardrail up and down, and also

from end to end. It should fit about $\frac{1}{2}$ inch inside the end baluster caps. Screw through the guardrail into the baluster caps, then nail through the guardrail trim into the guardrail itself, using 2-inch siding nails.

16 Trim the handrails. Glue and screw the handrail trim under the outside lip of the handrail. Clamp the trim in place while you drive the 2-inch screws up into the handrail itself. The trim not only stiffens the handrail, it also creates a shadow reveal that defines the architecture of the construction.

Trim the handrails. Glue and clamp the handrail trim under the outside lip of the handrail. Screw it to the handrail.

ARBOR WITH SEAT

Charming construction improves with age

An arbor with a seat is one of those garden accessories that can only improve with age. The vines creep up the side trellis, the tree branches poke through, the posts become buried in leaves. The arbor becomes part of the landscape, inviting you to rest, listen to the breeze, and renew yourself.

This arbor features a semicircular arch, which you jigsaw and assemble from small pieces of wood. Because rectangular keys join the circular segments, there are no critical angles or difficult joints. Horizontal pieces called capitals connect the arched top to the upright posts. This allows you to tailor the width of the arbor by changing the length of the capitals.

The arbor consists of five discrete assemblies: the arched top, the two side panels, the seat, and the back. These assemblies bolt together, which allows you to make them in the workshop, then carry the parts outdoors to reassemble in their final location. It also allows you to disassemble your arbor for winter storage or for moving.

The upright posts are three-piece composites, and so is the front seat beam. This method of construction is very strong, simple and light. The arch top, the back and the bench seat work together to keep the assembly square.

DETAIL OF ARCHED TOP

The six arch segments are identical segments of a circular ring.

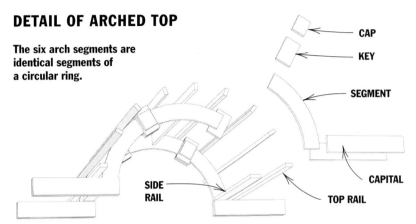

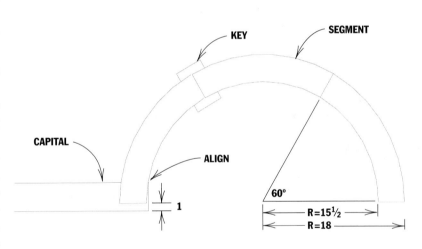

BUILDING THE ARBOR

1 Cut the wood. Begin by sawing all of the wood to length. This way you can work around knots and defects, and get the most mileage out of your materials budget. It's important to make all the pieces of the arbor in clear wood, with small knots or no knots.

2 Lay out the arch. Each semicircular arch consists of three segments, connected by two rectangular keys. You must lay out the arch full-size, either on a big piece of paper, or directly on the top of the worktable, as shown in the photo on page 93. Then lay out each segment on the full-

ARBOR WITH SEAT

ARCHED TOP ASSEMBLY

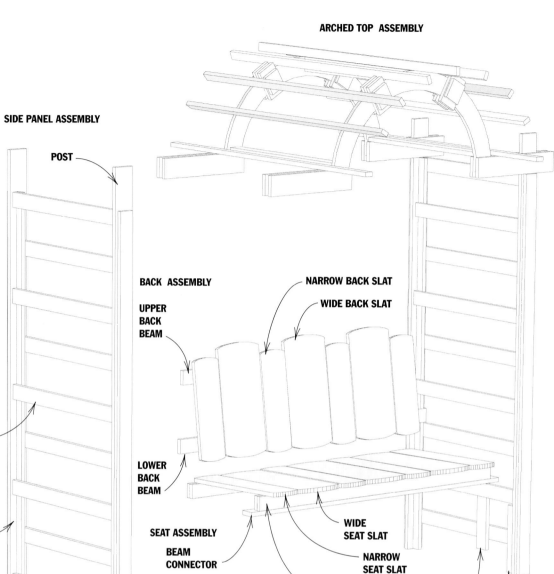

SIDE PANEL ASSEMBLY

POST

BACK ASSEMBLY

NARROW BACK SLAT

WIDE BACK SLAT

UPPER BACK BEAM

SIDE RAIL

INSIDE POST FACE

LOWER BACK BEAM

SEAT ASSEMBLY

BEAM CONNECTOR

WIDE SEAT SLAT

NARROW SEAT SLAT

SEAT BEAM

OUTSIDE POST FACE

SEAT BRACE

RAIL BRACE

Construct the arbor in five sections: arched top, two side panels, seat, and back. Begin by assembling two arches from the segments, keys and capitals, then connect the arches with the top rails to complete the arched top. Make the four post assemblies and connect them with the side rails, making the two side panels. Screw the seat slats to the seat beams, and the back slats to the back beams. Then assemble the arbor, drill the bolt holes, and bolt the sections together.

Hex-head bolts join the seat and back to the posts.

YOUR INVESTMENT

Time: One weekend
Money: $110

SHOPPING LIST

24 feet 1×10 pine
24 feet 1×6 pine
48 feet 1×4 pine
96 feet 1×3 pine
72 feet 1×2 pine
#6 × 1¼-inch galvanized screws
#6 × 2-inch galvanized screws
2½-inch galvanized siding nails
2-inch galvanized siding nails
12 ¼ × 3-inch galvanized bolts
10 ¼ × 4-inch galvanized bolts

PROJECT SPECS

The arbor stands 78 inches high, 32 inches front to back, and 58 inches wide at the ground.

CUTTING LIST

PART	QTY.	DIMENSIONS	NOTES
ARCHED TOP			
Segment	6	¾ × 5½ × 22	1×6
Key	6	¾ × 5½ × 3 ½	1×6
Capital	8	¾ × 3½ × 18	1×4
Cap	8	¾ × 3½ × 3	1×4
Top rail	9	¾ × 1½ × 55	1×3
SIDE PANEL			
Post	4	¾ × 3½ × 78	1×4
Outside post face	4	¾ × 2½ × 71	1×3
Inside post face	4	¾ × 1½ × 71	1×2
Side rail	21	¾ × 2½ × 29	1×3
SEAT			
Wide seat slat	3	¾ × 9½ × 24	1×10
Narrow seat slat	4	¾ × 5½ × 24	1×6
Seat beam	4	¾ × 2½ × 54	1×3
Beam connector	1	¾ × 2½ × 54	1×3
Seat brace	2	¾ × 2½ × 12	1×3
Rail brace	2	¾ × 1½ × 12	1×2
BACK			
Wide back slat	3	¾ × 9½ × 20	1×10
Narrow back slat	4	¾ × 9½ × 18	1×6
Upper back beam	1	¾ × 2½ × 54⅜	1×3
Lower back beam	1	¾ × 2½ × 58	1×3

size drawing. After you've drawn the semicircular arch itself, divide it into 60-degree sectors with the protractor. You'll be able to lay out and jigsaw each of the six segments within a 22-inch board, as shown in the photo at right.

3 Saw the segments. While it's possible to tether the jigsaw to a center point in order to saw mechanically perfect arcs, it's hardly necessary. You can saw the segments freehand without worrying, because nothing is critical. Clamp each segment to the worktable and saw the outside curve, reclamp it to saw the inside curve, then saw both ends. Be careful you don't clamp

Lay out the arch. Make a stick compass to draw the semicircular arch full-size. Divide the semicircle into 60-degree segments, then transfer the drawing onto six pieces of 1×6 wood.

the line of the cut over the worktable itself, as shown below, or you might saw into it. Keep the curved scrap to use as a template in Step 13.

4 Join the arch. The keys join the segments of the arch. Assemble three of the segments on the full-size drawing. Draw a layout line down the center of

the keys, as shown below left, then locate the first key on a joint line. It should extend an inch beyond each side of the curve. Spread glue as shown below right, drill four clearance holes and screw the key to the segments with 1¼ inch screws. Make the second joint in the same way, then turn the assembly over to glue and screw a sec-

ond key on the back side of each joint, using the 2-inch screws. Make the second arch now too.

5 Add the capitals. The four capitals attached to each arch will make the bridge to the uprights. Set the parts in position on the worktable. The bottom edge of each capital should overhang the arch by 1 inch, with the top corner of the capitals meeting the inside curve of the arch, as shown in the photo at right. Use the edge of the worktable to keep the capitals in line. Spread glue on the intersections and drive three 1¼-inch screws through the arch and into each of the first two capitals. Turn the assembly over to attach the second pair of capitals on the other side, using the 2-inch screws. Join the remaining four capitals to the other arch in the same way.

6 Cap the keys. The caps are small blocks of 1×3 glued and nailed cross-grain on the keys. They reinforce the joints, and

Saw the segments. Steer the jigsaw around the curved layout lines, then saw the 60-degree mitered ends.

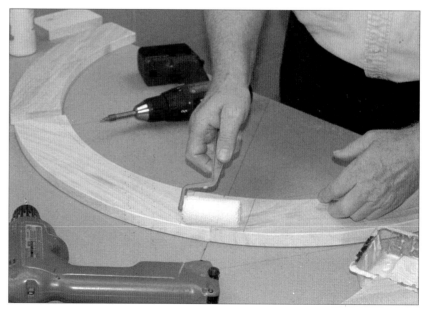

Join the arch. Draw a centerline on the key (above). Roll glue on the joint, and screw the pieces together (right).

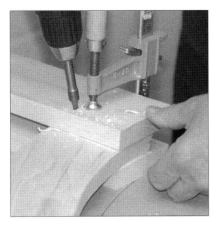

Add the capitals. The straight capitals overhang the arch by an inch, but they are flush at the inside top.

Cap the keys. Spread glue on the caps, center them atop the keys, and nail them in place.

they cover the screw holes. Spread glue on each cap in turn and center it on its key, as shown in the top center photo. Attach each cap with two or three of the 2-inch siding nails.

7 Connect the arches. Three side rails connect the two arch assemblies. Two of these pieces fit tight between the arches themselves, flat on the inside ends of the capitals, as shown in the photo at right. Drill clearance holes and drive two of the 2½-inch screws through the face of the arch into each end of the rails, then toenail a third screw through the rail into the capital below. The third rail fits between the arches at the top.

8 Top rails complete the arches. The nine 1×2 top rails make an open pattern against the sky. The top rails stand on edge atop the arches, attached with a 2½-inch screw at each intersection. Each top rail extends 12 inches beyond the outside face of the arch. One top rail goes on center atop the arches, four of them go one rail thickness on either side of the keys, two more sit at the midpoint between the keys and the

Connect the arches. Fit the two side rails on top of the capitals, tight against the inside of the arch. Screw through the segments, then screw down into the capitals. The last rail fits between the summits of the arches.

capitals, and two sit a rail thickness outside the base of the arches, atop the capitals. Use a 6½-inch spacer block to locate the midpoint rail, as shown in the photo at right

9 Nail the inside post faces to the posts. The composite post assemblies each consist of a 1×4 post, a 1×2 inside post face and a 1×3 outside post face. The height of the posts is somewhat arbitrary; if you deviate from the cutting list, make your post faces 7 inches shorter than your posts. Begin by rolling glue on

Top rails complete the arches. Arrange the top rails around the outside of the arches, using a scrap of wood to make uniform spaces.

Nail the inside post faces to the posts. Glue and clamp the inside post face to the post, then nail the parts together.

Attach the side rails to the posts. The side rails alternate from one side of the post faces to the other. A scrap of wood helps to maintain the uniform spacing between the side rails.

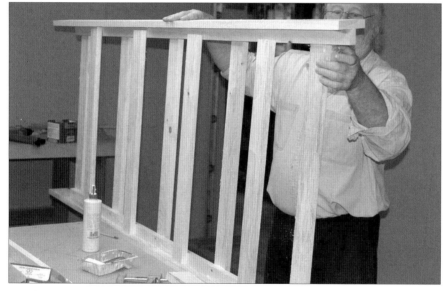

Complete the side panels. Dab glue onto the free ends of the rails, then wiggle the second post assembly into place. Square each rail before you screw it to the inside post face. Nail through the posts into the end-grain of each side rail.

of the first rail and fit it flush with the top of the inside post face. Tack it in place with one $1\frac{1}{4}$-inch screw. Use a $5\frac{1}{2}$-inch block of wood as a gauge to space the next rail down the post. Glue and screw it to the other side of the inside post face. Continue in this manner to the bottom of the post, where you'll have a space of about 4 inches to the ground. Attach the nine remaining side rails to another of the post assemblies in exactly the same way.

11 Complete the side panels. Now you can plug the remaining two post assemblies onto the free ends of the side rails. Spread glue on the side rails, then wiggle each post assembly into place, as shown at left. Use a framing square to adjust the position of each rail, then screw it to the inside post face. Finally, drive two $2\frac{1}{2}$-inch siding nails through the outside of the posts into the end grain of each side rail. Complete the second side panel in the same way.

one edge of an inside post face. Center it on the post by eye, with one end flush with what will be the bottom of the post, and clamp the two pieces together. Then nail through the post into the inside post face with 2-inch siding nails spaced about 12 inches apart, as shown in the photo at top left. Assemble the other three posts

and inside post faces in the same way.

10 Attach the side rails to the posts. Nine side rails connect each pair of posts, forming the two ladder-like side panels. The side rails alternate from one side of the inside post face to the other, as shown in the photo at top right. Spread glue on the end

12 Nail the outside post faces to the posts. Whereas the inside post faces fit the posts edge-on, the outside post faces fit face-on. Roll glue onto the broad side of an outside post face. Center it on the post by eye, flush at the bottom end. Nail through the outside post face into the post with the 2-inch siding nails spaced about a foot apart. Attach the other outside post faces in the same way.

13 Shape the seat and back slats. The seat and back slats have a jigsawn curve on both ends, as shown in the drawing below right. These curves are the same on all the slats, wide or narrow. As a template for laying out the curves, choose a regular piece of scrap left over from when you sawed the arch segments. Sand the template smooth. Trace the template onto both ends of all the seat and back slats. Since the template is a circular segment, the curve will be symmetrical if you square its straight edge with the edge of the slat, as shown in the photo at right. Jigsaw the curves, and use 80-grit sandpaper to remove any stray splinters of wood. Sand the sharp edges off the slats as well.

14 Make the seat beams. The front and rear seat beams each consist of two pieces of seat-beam material glued and screwed together. Make the joint with six 1¼-inch screws. The front seat beam has a beam connector piece glued and screwed onto its edge, as shown in the photo at far right. Center the seat beam from end to end on the beam connector, but make it

flush along one edge. Join these pieces with six 2-inch screws.

15 Assemble the seat. The seat slats alternate wide-narrow across the seat beams. There's clearance for the posts of 1⅝ inch at either end of the beams. The slats overhang the front beam by 3 inches. At the other end, they're flush with the edge of the rear seat beam. Square the two end slats across

the beams and clamp them in position, as shown in the top photo on the next page. Nail them to the beams with three 2½-inch siding nails at each end. Center and nail the middle seat slat, then fill in the remaining spaces with the remaining slats. There should be a space of about ⅛ inch between the slats.

16 Bolt the seat to the side panels. Stand the side panels

Shape the seat and back slats.
Square the scrap template across the end of the slat, then trace its shape.

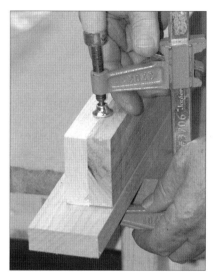

Make the seat beams. Glue and screw the seat beams together, then attach the front seat beam to the beam connector. Center the beam end to end.

SLAT DETAIL

Use the scrap from sawing the arch as a template for the seat and back slats.

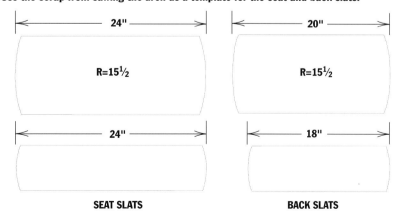

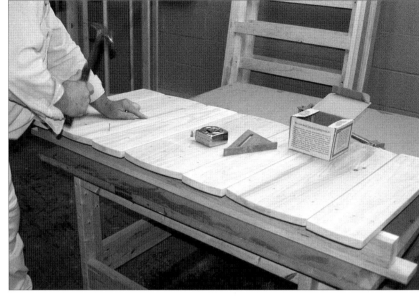

Assemble the seat. Clamp two narrow seat slats at the ends of the seat beams, leaving clearance for the posts. The front overhang is 3 inches (above). Nail the seat slats to the seat beams (right).

Bolt the seat to the side panels. Drill through the beam connector and side rail (above), then bolt the parts together (below).

upright and drop the seat into position. The seat beams rest on the second side rail up from the floor, with the rear seat beam tight in the pocket formed by the upright and side rail. Drill two $\frac{1}{4}$-inch bolt holes through each rear outside post face and post, and through the rear seat beams, as shown in the photo at left. It's important to bolt through as much wood as possible, which means you must drill the bolt holes on a slight angle. Drill another pair of $\frac{1}{4}$-inch bolt holes down through the ends of the beam connector and the side rail on which it rests. Fit 4-inch galvanized bolts through all the bolt holes, and thread them with nuts and washers.

17 Fit the back beams. The upper and lower back beams fit between the uprights. The back slats will be screwed to them in the next step. The top back beam fits in between the inside post faces, in line with the bottom of the fifth side rail, as shown in the top photo on the facing page. Clamp it in place and drill four bolt holes through the outside post face and post,

as in the previous step. Bolt the upper back beam in position. The lower back beam rests on top of the third side rail. It can be bolted right through all three components of the uprights, with two bolts in each end.

18 Attach the back slats. The seven back slats span the two back beams and are screwed to the beams from behind. There's a space between the bottom of the back slats and the seat, as shown in the top right photo on the facing page. Align each back slat with the corresponding seat slat. Drive the first $1\frac{1}{4}$-inch screw through the upper back beam, then square the slat to the beams before driving the second screw through the lower back beam. The two back beams are not in the same plane, which gives the back slats their comfortable slope. Lay out all the screws so they fall near the edges of the beams that bear against the slats.

19 Support the seat. The seat rests on the second side rail up from the ground. The seat brace and rail brace guarantee solid

Fit the back beams. Fit top back beam flush with the bottom of the fifth side rail, and bolt it (above). Bolt the lower back beam to the post assembly (right).

Attach the back slats. Block the back slats up on scrap (above). Screw them to the back beams from behind (below).

support. Glue and screw a rail brace under the front end of the side rails, in the vertical pocket formed by the post and inside post face. Then screw a seat brace vertically under each end of the front seat beam, as shown in the bottom left photo.

20 Assemble the arbor. Begin final assembly by fitting the seat and back between the side panels. Tap all the bolts home and tighten the nuts with a socket wrench. Enlist a helper to support the arched top while you wiggle the top ends of the post in between the four pairs of capitals. Fit one end, then fit the other end. Center the arched top from side to side, and pull the capitals down tight on the ledges atop the the post faces. Drill two ¼-inch holes through each intersection, as shown in the bottom right photo, and bolt the arbor together.

21 Install the arbor. Choose a lovely spot for your arbor, where you have vines and trees. Level the posts with bricks or flat rocks. Relax and contemplate the marvels of nature.

Support the seat. Glue and screw a brace under the front end of the rail that supports the seat. Fasten a second brace directly under the front seat beam.

Assemble the arbor. Drill holes for two bolts through the capitals and posts. Put a washer under the hex head and also under the nut.

SAWS AND SAWING

There are four basic kinds of sawing: Crosscutting, or sawing to length; ripping, or sawing to width lengthwise; mitering, or sawing at an angle, and sawing curves. Most of the time you want the sawn piece of wood to end up at some particular size, with its surfaces reasonably flat and smooth. And you often want more than one piece sawn to the same size.

For outdoor projects and general woodworking around the house, perhaps 90% of saw work is crosscutting to length.

Mitering the wood is just crosscutting at an angle other than 90 degrees. While it is handy to be able to rip to width, it's usually not absolutely necessary because you can buy wood in 1-inch increments of width. Most of the projects in this book have been designed around standard widths of lumber.

For making straight cuts, there are six basic types of saw: handsaw, jigsaw, portable circular saw, chop saw, bandsaw and table saw. Which ones you choose depend upon your bud-

get, your skill level, and how involved in woodworking you intend to become. You can take care of all your sawing needs with a $20 handsaw, along with sandpaper to knock the splinters off the cut. Or you could spend more than $1,000 for a cabinetmaker's table saw.

In terms of safety and skill, the important distinction is whether you move the saw over stationary wood, or move the wood over a stationary saw. It's generally safer to clamp the wood in one place and to move

SAWHORSE

If you're just starting out, a pair of sawhorses can be the foundation of your workshop: Throw a sheet of plywood across them, and you've got your first worktable. Carry them out onto the deck, and you've got a beautiful open-air workshop.

These sawhorses are made of standard 1× lumber, held together with glue and screws. The dimensions given in the drawing make a horse that's 24 inches high, about right to use with a portable circular saw or jigsaw. For handsawing, change the length of the legs to about 18 inches. To support a worktable, make 28-inch legs. The length of the sawhorse top is up to you.

The only angled cut in the sawhorse is the gusset. The angle is about 20 degrees, but the precise measurement mat-

ters less than making all four gussets the same.

Begin by gluing and screwing a gusset onto each pair of legs. Then set the leg-and-gusset assemblies upside-down on a flat surface in order to connect them with the rail. This ensures that their top surfaces will all be in the same plane. Next, glue and screw the top of the sawhorse to the rail and gussets, allowing it to overlap at the ends. Screw right down through the top and bury the screwheads in the wood. The second set of gussets, glued and screwed outside the legs, stiffens the construction.

Sawhorses give you a beachhead in the struggle to build up a workshop. They're extremely strong, yet they're direct and quick to make. Since they stack, you can make a herd as easily as a single pair, and they won't take up any more room in the shop.

Join gussets to legs. Align the top corner of the leg with the outside corner of the gusset. Glue and screw the parts together.

The rail connects the gussets. Center the rail on the leg-and-gusset assembly. Connect the parts with #6 × 2½-inch screws.

A handsaw is the only way to trim parts after they've been joined together.

the saw, as you do with the handsaw, portable circular saw, chop saw, and jigsaw. It's more accurate, too. When you move the wood over a stationary blade, such as a table saw, you're always at risk of losing control. It takes more skill to make safe and accurate cuts.

It might surprise you to hear that most people can quickly learn how to cut accurately with a handsaw. Even if you have a complete machine setup, you'll find a handsaw the only answer to some sawing

problems—trimming parts after they've become part of a larger construction, for example. It's also the easiest way to saw small notches and cutouts.

If you are beginning to woodwork around your house, you

do not need to make a major investment in sawing machinery. If you already have a table saw, fine, but if not, you can do very well with a handsaw or with a jigsaw. If you want a little more machine, consider a sliding-arm chop saw. It will handle all of your crosscutting and miter sawing, it's safe, and it's extremely accurate. The chop saw can't rip, so for the occasional lengthwise cut, and for breaking down sheets of plywood, you'll need a jigsaw or a portable circular saw as well.

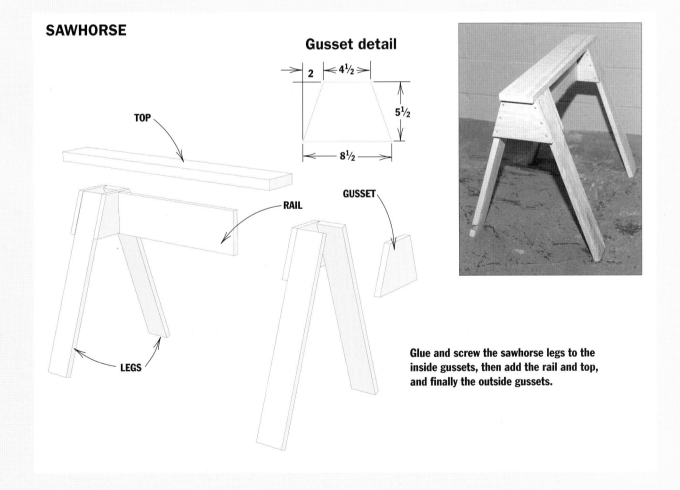

SAWHORSE

Gusset detail

TOP

RAIL

GUSSET

LEGS

Glue and screw the sawhorse legs to the inside gussets, then add the rail and top, and finally the outside gussets.

Handsaw

There's been a real change in handsaw technology in the last few years. Both Stanley and Sandvik now make a short toolbox saw with a new tooth profile derived from Japanese saws. The teeth are long and sharp, with a little triangular facet at the tip. They cut much more effectively than traditional handsaws, they're easier to start, and easier to control. If you have a choice, get the coarser saw, with eight or nine teeth to the inch.

Grip and stance are the keys to learning how to saw by hand. Wrap three fingers through the saw handle, with your index finger pointing along the blade, as shown in the photo at right. Tighten your thumb against your middle finger. Use a low saw horse, 18 inches is about right. This allows you to take a marching stance and to get your body over the work. The sawing motion comes from your shoulder, not your wrist or elbow. Align the saw with your wrist, arm and shoulder joint.

Hold the workpiece on the sawhorse with your left hand. If you can't easily keep it still, use your knee or a small clamp. Brace the sawblade with the thumb of your holding hand and start the cut with a couple of light backward strokes. This breaks the corner of the wood, and it also gets your body into alignment with the proposed cut. Then push, but don't force the saw. The saw's own weight is almost enough. If the saw jams, it may bend but it won't break. Saw with steady, even strokes.

Handsaw grip and stance. Wrap three fingers around the saw's handle and point your index finger along the blade. Sight straight down on the saw. Align the saw with your wrist, forearm and shoulder joint. To start the cut, brace the sawblade against the thumb of your holding hand. The sawing motion comes from the shoulder, not from the elbow or wrist.

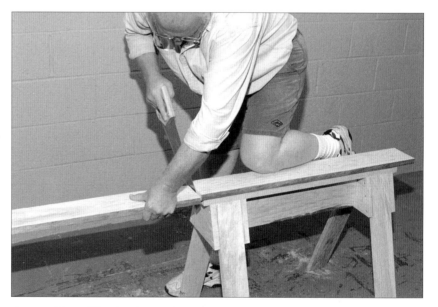

Crosscutting with a handsaw. To keep a long board from splintering at the end of the cut, reach over the saw and support it with your holding hand.

Handsaw crosscut. When you want to cut a long board in half, you'll need to support the offcut and keep it from falling, because otherwise it's liable to splinter. Clamp the workpiece to the sawhorse, or hold it with your knee, as shown in the photo above. Saw most of the way through the wood. When there's about an inch to go, reach around with your holding hand and take hold of the offcut. You'll be able to lift it free as the saw breaks through the last of the wood.

Handsaw rip. Unlike traditional saws, the new handsaws don't come in rip and crosscut versions. The same tooth profile works either way. To rip a board, draw a layout line on the wood. Clamp the workpiece to the sawhorse, stand beside it, and start to saw. When you come to the sawhorse, you'll have to unclamp the workpiece, move it along, and reclamp.

Handsaw miter. Mitering with a handsaw is the same as crosscutting. Draw a line, clamp the workpiece to the sawhorse, and start with short, backward strokes. Brace the saw with the thumb of your holding hand.

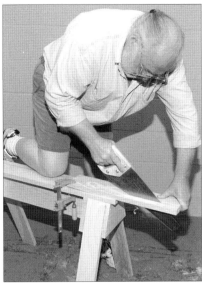

Ripping with a handsaw. Draw a layout line on the wood and clamp it to the sawhorse. Stand beside the sawhorse. Move and reclamp the wood as you progress. You may find it helpful to plant your knee on the sawhorse, so you can get your shoulder right over the saw.

JIGSAW

If you are beginning to woodwork in order to improve your home, a jigsaw is the least startling and most versatile saw you can buy. It's light, it's capable of reasonable accuracy, and it can saw everything, including curves. The blade is little and it goes up and down with a whirring noise, unlike circular saws which go around with a roar and a lot of wind. The jigsaw's disadvantage is the time it takes to set up each cut. There's no ready way to set up once and cut many parts.

If you're only going to have one power saw and you want to limit your investment, the jigsaw is your only choice. A good machine will cost about $150; look for a saw with a blade-guide bearing right above its sole plate. Low-priced saws have sloppy mechanisms and no guide bearings, so they do less accurate work. Be sure to use blades for cutting wood. Blades for metal

and plastic are also available, and they're often sold as a set.

Portable saws require cord management. You do not want to saw through the cord, nor do you want to be pulled up short in the middle of the cut. Always rehearse your cutting path before you turn on the saw. If you start the cut and the tool gets hung up, let go of the trigger and back up a half-inch, and look at

your setup to figure out what's causing the problem. Don't blindly push onward.

As with any other portable power tool or woodworking machine, always wear safety glasses with side shields whenever you use a jigsaw.

Jigsaw rip. While you can freehand the cut, you'll have much better results if you

You can make a rip jig for the jigsaw, as shown on page 105. Here the rip jig is clamped to a diagonal line, so it will make two tapered pieces of wood.

Mitering with a jigsaw. The crosscut jig clamped to the layout line guides the jigsaw. This cut will not have a splintered edge because it is "with the grain." The end of the board was cut from the opposite direction, with visible splintering.

Ripping with a jigsaw. Make a gauge stick, like the stick at the bottom right of the photo, whose width matches the distance from the edge of the jigsaw's sole to its blade. Use the gauge stick to locate and clamp a fence to the workpiece. Cut by pressing the saw against the fence.

clamp a fence to the workpiece. You have to offset the fence by the distance from the edge of the saw's sole to its blade, which you can do by direct measurement, or with a gauge. The gauge is a straight stick of wood whose width matches the jigsaw's sole-to-blade offset distance.

Begin by drawing the layout line on the workpiece. Then use the gauge to position the fence the offset distance away from the layout line. Clamp the fence to the workpiece. The jigsaw is a light tool, it's easy to control, so it's not necessary to clamp the workpiece to the sawhorse or worktable.

Always start the jigsaw before the blade contacts the workpiece, and ease it into the cut. Let the saw cut at its own

Crosscutting with a jigsaw. Use a gauge stick to position and clamp a fence to the workpiece, offset from the layout line. Make the cut by pressing the saw's sole against the fence.

speed. If you force it, you'll flex the blade and send it off the line. You can stop the saw at any time, but don't try to lift it out of the cut while it's running. Let it stop first.

Jigsaw crosscut and miter. The jigsaw is forgiving of grain direction, so crosscutting can be approached the same way as ripping. Position the fence with the gauge, clamp, and go.

JIGS FOR PORTABLE SAWS

A couple of simple jigs take all the guesswork out of ripping and crosscutting with jigsaws and portable circular saws. The basic jig consists of a fence attached to a baseplate. The saw rides on the baseplate, guided by the fence. The first time you use one of these jigs, the saw cuts through the baseplate. Every time thereafter, the saw automatically cuts right along the edge of the baseplate.

Jigs for jigsaws are the same as jigs for the portable circular saw. The only difference is the distance from the jig's fence to the edge of the baseplate, which has to match the distance from the saw blade to the edge of the jigsaw's sole. If you use the saw to trim the jig, it comes out right.

It's tempting to imagine a universal jig for portable saws, one that would make every cut. But in any specific situation, such a jig would never be the right size. It's better to make more than one jig. Make a rip jig for pieces up to 4 feet long. The first time you need to rip a longer piece of wood, you might make an 8-foot jig, but you might go for years without ever getting to that point. Make a 16-inch crosscut jig for ordinary sizes of 1× and 2× lumber. You can also use the crosscut jig for sawing miters.

The rip jig consists of a 4-foot fence made from 1×3 or 1×4 pine, glued and screwed to a baseplate, which is a 4-foot by 6-inch strip of ¼-inch Masonite. Glue and screw the pine fence to the baseplate with ¾-inch screws; Masonite soaks up glue,

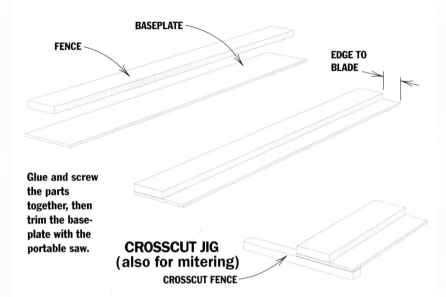

RIP JIG

FENCE

BASEPLATE

EDGE TO BLADE

Glue and screw the parts together, then trim the baseplate with the portable saw.

CROSSCUT JIG (also for mitering)

CROSSCUT FENCE

Trim the baseplate. Clamp the jig to a piece of wood atop the sawhorse. Saw the baseplate with the portable circular saw or the jigsaw.

Make the crosscut fence. Glue and screw the crosscut fence to the bottom of the jig's baseplate. Align the parts with a square, drive the first screw, then align them again before driving the second screw.

so roll two wet coats onto it.

To trim the baseplate to the exact width of the saw's sole, clamp the jig to a piece of wood so the cut is supported, and with the saw's sole riding against the pine fence, saw the baseplate from one end to the other. Now the jig is ready to use.

Make the crosscut jig in exactly the same way as you made the rip jig, but make the

pine fence and the Masonite baseplate 16 inches long. The crosscut fence is a 9-inch length of 1×2 pine. Glue and screw it to the bottom of the jig. The trick is making the crosscut fence square to the edge of the baseplate. To do that, spread the glue and align the parts with your square, as shown in the photo above. Drill a pilot hole and drive one screw. Then square up the parts again, before you drill and drive the second screw.

PORTABLE CIRCULAR SAW

The portable circular saw is an inexpensive way to get started in power-tool woodworking. However, you can't get far with the bare saw. You need to invest time in making jigs.

There are several styles of saw. The main choice is whether the motor is to the right of the blade or to the left. Left-mounted saws are new on the market, and they are easier to use because a right-handed person has a better view of the line of cut. Expect to spend about $150. Cheap saws may not be well engineered and won't be sturdy. If you spend much more than $150, you're into professional grade, worm-drive machines that are liable to be too heavy. Be sure to get a carbide blade.

Like routers and jigsaws, portable circular saws require cord management. Drape the cord so you won't saw through it, and so it won't catch someplace in the middle of the cut.

All portable circular saws have a spring-loaded blade guard. The guard has a hand lever that allows you to lift it out of the way to start the cut. It snaps back into place as soon as the saw leaves the workpiece. However, there is no guard underneath the workpiece, where the blade breaks through. This is why it is critically important always to clamp the workpiece to the sawhorse or worktable, and to keep both hands on the saw. If you try to handhold the workpiece, you are liable to curl your fingers into the path of the whirling blade.

Ripping with a portable circular saw. Make a rip jig and clamp it to the workpiece, with the edge of its Masonite baseplate on your layout line. Run the sole of the saw along the jig's fence. Here the saw is ripping a 2×2 from the edge of a 2×6.

Crosscutting with a portable circular saw. Make a crosscut jig and clamp it to the workpiece. The jig's crosscut fence keeps the cut square.

Portable circular saw rip. To rip, or saw the wood lengthwise, clamp a fence to the workpiece so that the edge of the fence guides the portable circular saw along the line you wish to cut. This means offsetting the fence by the distance from the saw blade to the edge of its sole. You can do it by measurement, with a gauge as discussed on page 105, or with the jig shown above.

Note, that you have to allow for the width of the saw blade itself, which is called the saw kerf. If the workpiece is the part of the wood that's clamped under the jig, it's no problem. If the workpiece is the falling board, be sure to offset the jig ⅛ inch to compensate for the kerf.

It takes a little practice to get good results with a portable circular saw. Pay attention to keeping the saw level, with its sole pressed down flat on the workpiece or jig, and tight against the fence. The usual error is to inadvertently tilt the saw, but if you pay attention and make a few practice cuts, you'll soon learn how to get it right.

Portable circular saw crosscut. While it's possible to free-hand a crosscut with the portable circular saw, you'll have much better results if you make the jig described on page 105. The jig has a crosscut fence, in addition to the fence that actually guides the saw. The crosscut fence aligns the jig square to the edge of the workpiece. Clamp the edge of the jig's base right on the layout line.

Portable circular saw miter. Mitering, or sawing angles, is essentially the same as crosscutting and uses the same jig. Use the corner of the crosscut fence to position the jig on the layout line. Saw slowly and carefully.

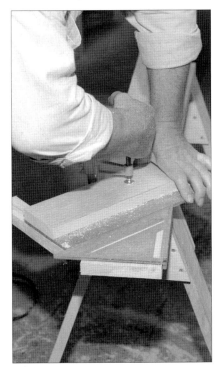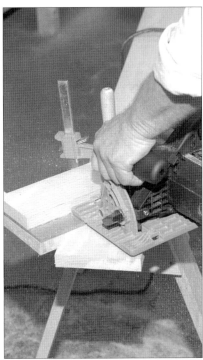

Mitering with a portable circular saw. Clamp the crosscut jig to the layout line. A carpenter's speed square can help you clamp the jig at 45 degrees (left). Guide the sole of the saw along the fence of the jig. Press the saw down level on the jig's baseplate (right).

CHOP SAW

Since most sawing for household projects is crosscutting to length, the chop saw is an excellent choice of machine. With a carbide-tipped saw blade, it makes a superb cut, accurate and clean. Since the saw moves while the wood remains stationary, the chop saw is a relatively safe machine, provided you don't attempt to disable its built-in blade guard. Crosscutting and mitering is all the chop saw can do, so you'll need another way to rip wood to width, such as a jigsaw.

There are two kinds of chop saw, pivoting, and sliding arm. With either type of saw, always cut with the workpiece extending to the left of the blade, and the waste to the right. Hold the

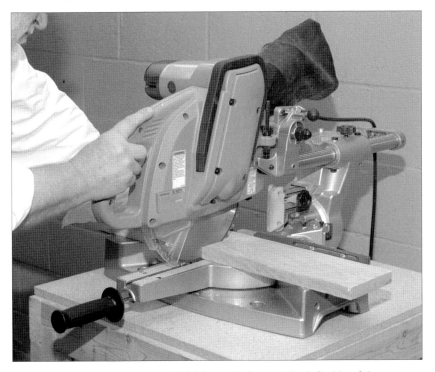

Crosscutting with a chop saw. Hold the workpiece on the left side of the saw blade, with the offcut to the right. With a sliding-arm chop saw, pull the blade forward of the workpiece, then lower it and push it to the back.

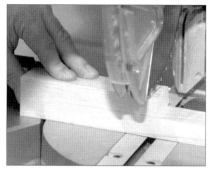

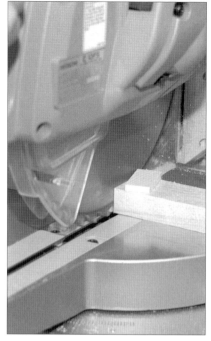

Crosscutting multiples. To saw two pieces the same length, align one piece of wood on top of the second piece. With the saw off, bring the lay-out line over to the blade (above). Chop through both pieces at once (center). To saw many pieces to an exact length, clamp an auxiliary fence to the chop saw's fence, and clamp a stop block to it. Butt each workpiece against the stop block (below).

Mitering with a chop saw. Rotate the saw table to the miter angle. To miter at a precise length, make a layout line on the workpiece (above) and make a shallow cut to the right of it. This shows you where the saw is cutting, so you can shift the work to it and chop through (below).

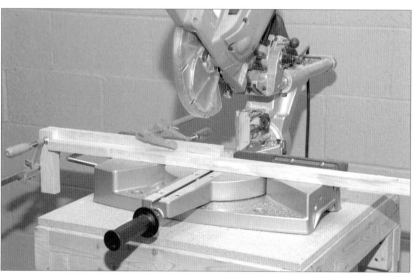

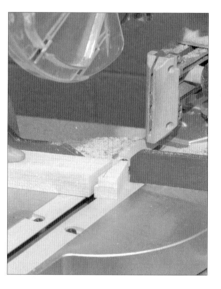

work with your left hand and drive the saw with your right hand. This method gives you the best view of the layout line. With a pivoting saw, the blade pulls down into the wood. With a sliding-arm saw, the blade pivots down and moves forward and backward. Always bring the blade forward of the work and push it through the wood to the back. This takes advantage of the saw's cutting force to push the work into the saw fence.

Always wear a face shield, safety goggles, or safety glasses with side shields whenever you use a chop saw.

Chop saw crosscut. The chop saw is designed to crosscut. Make your layout line on the wood and press it against the fence. With your fingers carefully away from the ON trigger, lower the saw and align the edge of one sawtooth with the layout line. Move the work along the

fence until the layout line is exactly to the left of the saw blade. Make sure none of your fingers are near the line of the cut before you pull the trigger on the saw. Pull it down and push it through the wood.

Chop saw multiples. To make two pieces the same size, saw one end of both pieces, but make sure both are still oversize. Draw a layout line on one piece and put it on top of the other piece, with their cut ends to the left of the saw blade. Align the cut ends with your left hand, while you bring the layout mark up to the saw blade as shown in the photos at left. Then crosscut both pieces at once.

To crosscut multiple pieces to an exact size, make an auxiliary fence with a stop block, and clamp it to the regular chop saw fence, as shown in the bottom left photo on the previous page. However, saw the first end on all the workpiece wood before you attach the auxiliary fence to the saw. Then butt the sawn end against the stop block and go.

Chop saw miter. The chop saw is ideal for mitering. Most models have a rotating saw table.

Whenever possible, rotate the saw table to keep the workpiece on the left of the blade. To miter to a given length, mark the length on the wood and begin the cut $\frac{1}{4}$ inch to the right of the mark. Cut part-way through the wood, just far enough to see the cut against the layout line. Now you can sneak up on the line by moving the workpiece to the right.

TABLE SAW

You can do an amazing number of operations with a table saw. However, what it does best is rip wood to width, and with a suitable jig or miter fence it can also crosscut it to length or to a given angle.

If you are shopping for a table saw, look at a mid-priced contractor-style machine with a 10-inch blade, about $750. It will be more accurate than an 8-inch benchtop saw. The motor of a contractor-style saw hangs off the back of the machine and drives the blade by means of a vee belt. On a benchtop saw, the blade mounts directly on the saw motor. This arrangement limits the thickness of wood the saw can cut.

All new table saws come with some kind of blade guard. Some guards work beautifully, but some are unwieldy. If your saw has an awkward guard, it is a serious mistake to remove it and work without it. The right answer is to look for an after-market guard that suits you, or to design and make one that really does work well. Take the problem of guarding your saw as a challenge, not as a nuisance. Likewise, always wear a face

PUSH STICK

A pair of push sticks allows you to propel wood past the table saw blade without risking your fingers. Always make push sticks in pairs, and keep one on the left side of the saw table, and one on the right, where they're easy to grab. It's important to make simple push sticks, because there can't be anything in the way of making new ones whenever you need them. If the saw chews one up, it has served its purpose well—chuck it and make another. The push stick

Make the notch with a handsaw.

shown here is made from a 12-inch cutoff of 1×2 pine. You can handsaw the notch, or saw it with a jigsaw.

PUSH STICK $\frac{1}{2}$ — 12 — 1½ — 90°

shield, safety goggles or safety glasses with side shields.

Table saw rip. Ripping, or sawing the wood lengthwise in order to make it narrower, is a safe and straightforward operation. The fence should be parallel to the saw blade, and on its right-hand side. The workpiece is the portion of the wood between the fence and the blade; the falling board or offcut is the piece of wood to the left of the blade.

Raise the blade so the bottom of the gullets between the sawteeth clear the top surface

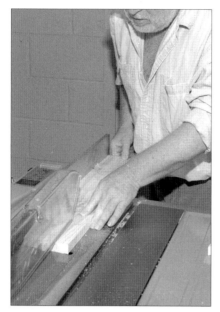

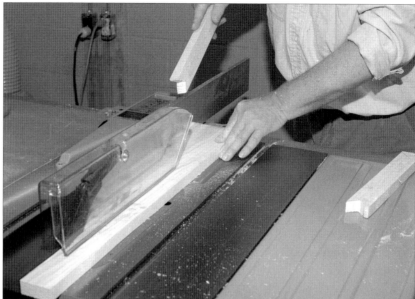

Ripping with a table saw. Stand alongside the wood, not directly behind it. The right hand propels the wood forward into the blade. The left hand holds it down on the table (above). When the back end of the wood reaches the saw table, pause and pick up your push sticks (top right). The splitter, behind the sawblade, keeps the cut from closing and kicking back. Complete the cut with the push sticks. Push the workpiece and the falling board completely past the blade (right).

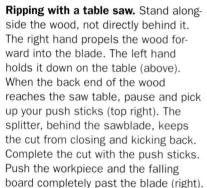

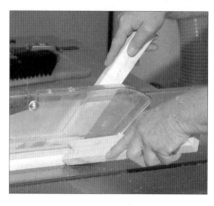

Crosscutting with a table saw. Hold the wood tight against the miter gauge and push the gauge past the saw blade.

of the wood. Set the width before you switch on the power. Make a pair of push sticks, as shown in the drawing on the previous page, and keep them handy, one on the left side of the saw table, one on the right. If the board is longer than about 6 feet, set up an outfeed support to catch it.

For safe ripping, regardless of the style of blade guard your saw has, you must use a splitter. The splitter is a metal plate attached to the saw structure on the back side of the blade. If the wood were to distort, it would keep the sawblade from kicking the wood back at the operator.

To feed the wood, stand in front of the saw, but to the left of

the blade. Make sure the wood is not touching the blade when you turn on the power. Lift the back of the board so its leading end is down tight on the saw table. Feed steadily and evenly, and pay attention to the contact between the fence and the workpiece. When the back end of the board reaches the saw table, pick up one push stick and then the other, both of which you left conveniently placed before you turned on the saw. Propel the tail of the board past the blade with a push stick in each hand, not with your fingers.

Table saw crosscut. Crosscut with the aid of the miter gauge, a T-shaped tool that rides in

grooves in the saw table. Move the rip fence completely out of the way to the right of the blade. The head of the miter gauge is only about 7 inches wide, but you can extend it by bolting an auxiliary fence of wood onto it.

Set the gauge to 90 degrees on its scale, but don't rely on it. Crosscut a piece of wood and check it with your try square. Adjust the gauge accordingly. Make sure the locking knob is tight before you cut. At the end of the cut, as soon as the wood has been severed, pull it away from the blade to the left, before you pull the miter gauge back. Remove the cutoff with your push stick. Don't reach over the blade with your hand.

Table saw multiples. To crosscut multiple pieces, set up a stop block to the right of the blade. Make sure the workpiece entirely clears the stop block before it touches the blade. Otherwise, the wood can get trapped between the blade and stop block, and it will be thrown back at you. One safe way to do this is to clamp a block of wood to the rip fence, as shown in the photo above right. The block must be big enough to keep the workpiece from being trapped between the rip fence and the blade, even if the workpiece were to pivot diagonally. This is the only time you can use the rip fence in conjunction with the miter gauge.

Another way to saw multiples is to clamp a stop block onto an auxiliary fence attached to the miter gauge, as shown in the center photo. The workpiece is to the left of the blade, and the offcut is to the right. Move the rip fence entirely out of the way.

Table saw miter. Table saw mitering is like crosscutting, except the wood tends to creep along the miter gauge. Prevent it from creeping by clamping it to an auxiliary fence attached to the miter gauge, as shown in the photo at right.

Crosscutting multiples. A stop block clamped to the rip fence allows you to crosscut multiple parts to the same length. The stop block must be at the front of the saw table, not near the sawblade. It must be wide enough that the workpiece cannot become trapped between the sawblade and the rip fence (top). The stop block can be clamped to an auxiliary fence that is screwed to the miter gauge. In this setup, move the rip fence entirely out of the way (above).

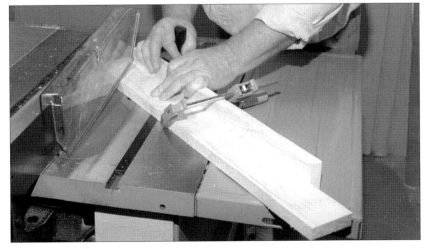

Mitering on a table saw. Miter with an auxiliary fence screwed or bolted to the miter gauge. To keep the workpiece from creeping, clamp it to the auxiliary fence.

CAMBIUM PRESS

PO Box 9 ... USA
phone 20 ... 3 2785
WWW.CAM...

FURNITURE PROJECTS FOR THE DECK AND LAWN
Attractive 2x4 Woodworking Projects Anyone Can Build

John Kelsey

Here are 16 sturdy, functional and attractive woodworking projects for the deck and lawn. Readers can make all of these handsome projects using ordinary 1-by and 2-by lumber, with basic woodwoking tools. Each project includes a detailed materials list, step-by-step instructions, and an assembly drawing showing how all the pieces fit. The parts connect with waterproof glue plus nails or screws -- this sturdy furniture goes together fast! The projects may be finsihed with paint or varnish, or they may be left unfinished to weather naturally. Readers will enjoy making these terrific outdoor projects, and their families will enjoy using the handsome results.

$14.95 ($22.95 in Canada)
Paperback / 112 pages / 8.5 x 11 / 16 complete projects
240 black-and-white photos, 42 drawings
ISBN 1-892836-17-3

WOODWORKER'S ESSENTIAL FACTS, FORMULAS & SHORT-CUTS
Rules of Thumb Help Figure It Out, With or Without Math

Ken Horner

Nearly every woodworking operation requires a fact, a calculation, or a reasonably close estimate. WOODWORKER'S ESSENTIAL shows how to solve woodworkingproblems by using math, or by following simple rules of thumb. With this fact-packed handbook on the bench, woodworkers can enjoy workshop success even if they are not comfortable making calculations.

list price, $24.95
Paperback / 312 pages / 8x10
400 black-and-white illustrations
ISBN 1-892836-15-7

THE NATURE AND ART OF WORKMANSHIP

David Pye

In a mechanized age, does it make any sense to work with hand tools when machines can do the same job? Cutting through a century of fuzzy thinking, Prof. Pye proposes a new theory based on the concepts of "workmanship of risk", and "workmanship of certainty."

list price $22.95
160 pgs, 8.5x11, b&w, pbk,
ISBN 0-9643999-0-3

SHOP DRAWINGS FOR CRAFTSMAN INTERIORS
Cabinets, Moldings & Built-Ins for Every Room in the Home

Measured & Drawn by Robert W. Lang

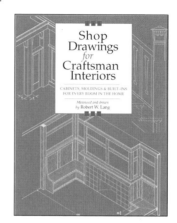

Stickley Craftsman-style homes, cottages and bungalows are among the most popular housing in America, and many books detail them in lovely color photos. This is the first and only book to present working shop drawings for carpenters and woodworkers who wish to repair or replace original Craftsman detailing, as well as for those who wish to create new work in the Craftsman style.

list price, $24.95
192 pages, 8.5 x 11, pbk
Hundreds of line drawings
ISBN 1-892836-16-5

SHOP DRAWINGS FOR CRAFTSMAN FURNITURE
27 Stickley Designs for Every Room in the Home

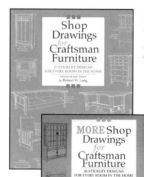

list price $22.95

144 pp, 8.5 x 11, b&w, pbk.
ISBN 1-892836-12-2

MORE SHOP DRAWINGS FOR CRAFTSMAN FURNITURE
30 Stickley Designs for Every Room in the Home

list price $22.95
144 pp, 8.5 x 11, b&w, pbk.
ISBN 1-892836-14-9

Robert W.Lang

Here, at last, are accurate shop drawings of Stickley Craftsman furniture. Woodworker Bob Lang has sought authentic Craftsman antiques for measuring. Each project is complete with dimensioned orthographic views, details and sections, plus a cutting list. Projects include tables, chairs, bureaus, armoires, bookcases, desks, and plant stands. Technical introduction.

APPEARANCE & REALITY:
A Visual Handbook for Artists, Designers, and Makers

Stephen Hogbin

This new design handbook goes beyond tired Modernism. Hogbin examines the fundamentals of line, form, color, and pattern, then moves on to investigate such broader issues as context, gender, community, region, the enviornment, and cultural diversity - which together govern the meaning conveyed by the made object. Essential for students and important for mature designers.

list price $29.95
192 pgs, 8.5 x 10, color, paperback, ISBN 1-892836-05-X